PARNELL AND HIS ISLAND

PARNELL AND HIS ISLAND

George Moore

edited by
Carla King

University College Dublin Press
Preas Choláiste Ollscoile Bhaile Átha Cliath

First published by Swan Sonnenschein,
Lowrey & Co, London, 1887
This edition first published by
University College Dublin Press 2004

Introduction and notes © Carla King 2004

ISBN 1-904558-16-X
ISSN 1393-6883

University College Dublin Press
Newman House, 86 St Stephen's Green
Dublin 2, Ireland
www.ucdpress.ie

Cataloguing in Publication data available from the British Library

Typeset in Ireland in Baskerville by Elaine Shiels, Bantry, Co. Cork
Printed on acid-free paper in Ireland by ColourBooks, Dublin

CONTENTS

INTRODUCTION.

Carla King

Few who have ever walked the Vico Road as it winds its way above Dublin Bay could fail to respond to the beguiling depiction of it with which Moore draws the reader into this book. We have the still mirror of water, the 'blue embaying mountains', seagulls, sailboats, villas, pine-trees, young girls in white dresses playing tennis—the idyll of a calm summer afternoon. But very soon, like the zooming in of a film camera, we are shown that the poetry of the vision masks the prosaic reality of decaying grandeur: 'The white walls shine in the sun and deceive you, but if you approach you will find a front-door where the paint is peeling, and a ruined garden.' And inside the door languishes an impoverished and parasitic gentry, struggling to maintain the appearance of respectability. The counterpoint between a landscape lovingly described with painterly precision and a society, poor, and morally bankrupt, lies at the centre of *Parnell and His Island*.

These essays first appeared separately under the title 'Lettres sur l'Irlande' as a series of six weekly articles in *Le Figaro*, 31 July to 4 September 1886, written originally in English but translated for publication in the paper.[1] They were published in volume form in French with some additions, as *Terre d'Irlande* early in 1887.[2] Moore experienced difficulty in finding a London publisher prepared to risk taking them on; finally Herbert Wigram, editor of Swann, Sonnenschein, agreed to bring out the book on condition that he be allowed to delete what he considered the most objectionable parts of the text.[3]

In June 1887 it appeared in English in a somewhat toned-down form (and with one amendment to the order of chapters) as *Parnell and His Island*.[4] In this edition of the book, the passages removed by Wigram have been replaced in the notes, in the French in which they appeared in *Terre d'Irlande*, and in English translation.

The origins of *Parnell and His Island* lie in two crises: one was the outbreak of the Land War between landlords and tenants. The last years of the 1870s were very difficult for farmers who endured a combination of harvest failures, brought on by adverse climatic conditions, and low prices caused by competition from producers in the New World. Irish tenant farmers faced the prospect of a sharp reduction in their incomes, throwing many, especially those on the small, impoverished farms in the West, into real hardship. In order to force landlords to reduce rents and deter them from evicting in the case of non-payment, the Irish National Land League of Mayo was founded in Castlebar, on 16 August 1879, less than twenty miles from the Moore family's estate. This was relaunched as a national organisation in Dublin two months later. The movement spread throughout the country, and was linked to a newly militant Home Rule Party in the House of Commons, with Charles Stewart Parnell becoming leader of both the parliamentary and popular organisations. Many of the League's leaders and activists were former Fenians who saw in the new body a more practical way of applying their energies after the unsuccessful rising of 1867. Its success greatly alarmed both government and landlords and it was effective in achieving rent reductions, although the number of evictions continued to rise; between 1879 and 1883 some 14,600 tenants were evicted.[5] Part of its novelty lay in the tactics it employed, which—at least in theory—were confined to passive resistance. Boycotting, stopping the hunt and peaceful demonstrations at the scene of evictions were all the more difficult for the authorities to deal with because they were not, in themselves, criminal activities. But however often its leaders deplored it, the popular mobilisation resulted in an increase in crime, traditional in many parts of the country in the form of agrarian 'outrage'. This varied from sending threatening letters, to mutilating livestock, damaging property or shooting landlords or their bailiffs. By 1880 the country was becoming ungovernable. Incidents of agrarian crime, which normally averaged around 200–300 per annum, rose to 863 in 1879, 2,585 in 1880 and 4,439 in 1881.[6] Frightened landlords remitted an estimated figure of at least £3 million of their rents, or perhaps one fifth of the total rental in 1879 and a further £4 million in the first seven months of 1880.[7] This was the beginning of a social revolution, what Michael Davitt called 'the fall of feudalism in Ireland', that would bring about the transfer of Irish land from some ten thousand landlords to approximately half a million tenants.

The outbreak of the land crisis brought another, more personal one for George Moore. He had been living happily as an absentee landlord in Paris, studying art, writing poetry and revelling in the vibrant cultural life of the city. He had become friendly with many of the leading French artists and writers of the time, and was a regular visitor to the Café Nouvelle Athènes, frequented by Impressionist painters such as Manet, Pissarro and Degas. He became particularly friendly with Edouard Manet, attending the evening gatherings in his studio and was painted by him several times (there are three extant portraits). Manet died on 30 April 1883, and *Terre d'Irlande* is dedicated to him: 'L'ami que nous aimions, le peintre dont nous adorons le génie.'[8]

Moore's life in Paris came to an abrupt end following a letter in August 1879 from his uncle, Joe Blake, who had been acting as his agent in Mayo. Blake wrote to say that the tenants were refusing to pay rents and that he was afraid to risk his life by serving eviction orders to collect them. Moreover, Moore had been allowed an advance that he could no longer recoup from rents and his uncle now wished to be repaid some £3,000. Blake added that, as he wished to give up the agency, Moore should come home to put his affairs in order and find a new agent. The letter threw Moore into a panic. With one of the 300 largest estates in Ireland and a nominal income of £3,596, the blow was unexpected. In *Confessions of a Young Man* (1889), he parodied his indignation that 'some wretched miners and farmers should refuse to starve that I may not be deprived of my demi-tasse at Tortoni's, that I may not be deprived of my beautiful retreat, my cat and my python—monstrous'.[9] Malcolm Brown claims that 'The traumatic shock of Blake's letter was the most memorable experience of Moore's life.'[10]

As a result of Blake's letter, Moore abandoned Paris and threw himself into writing. Paris had formed him intellectually and he mourned his break with it, but with no certainty that the tenants would ever pay rents again he believed that he would henceforth have to live on his earnings. For the next few years he moved between London, Dublin and Moore Hall, publishing four novels, a pamphlet and a considerable amount of journalism between 1883 and the appearance of *Parnell and His Island*.[11] He was to remain a hard-working and productive writer for the rest of his life.

Had Moore's only intention been to make money from his writings he would never have written the books he did. While in France, he had read widely in French literature, particularly the works of Balzac (which he claimed to know by heart),[12] Flaubert, and Zola, among many others. He was greatly influenced by Naturalism, of which Émile Zola was the chief exponent in France. According to the programme that Zola sketched out for the movement, writers should take their subjects from social reality, and preferably from the writer's own experience. Naturalists believed that people are conditioned by their surroundings and used description of milieux to explain their characters. They also paid close attention to portraying appearance, dress and behaviour, spheres in which Moore, with his keen memory for detail, excelled. They were influenced by Darwin's evolutionary theories in stressing the importance of hereditary characteristics in their characters and in emphasising the contiguity of man's instincts with those of animals.[13] Moore had known several writers of the Naturalist school in Paris, although he only became friendly with Zola in the early 1880s, after he had championed Naturalism in the British press and began a translation (never completed) of Zola's *L'Assommoir*. But with the publication of his first novels he emerged as the leading Naturalist writer in English. This brought him into immediate conflict with upholders of Victorian morality in the shape of the circulating libraries, W. H. Smith and Mudie's Select Library, which banned his books from their shelves. Thus, even before the publication of *Parnell and His Island*, Moore had already made his name as 'The bad boy of English literature', in Susan Mitchell's phrase.[14]

Moore returned to Ireland in the winter of 1880–1, when he stayed at Moore Hall and visited relatives in Mayo and Galway. He toured his property with Blake, met his tenants and appointed Tom Ruttledge as his new agent. The impressions gained on this return to Ireland and during subsequent sojourns during 1883–4 and 1884–5 form the basis for both *A Drama in Muslin* (1886) and *Parnell and His Island*.

A Drama in Muslin tells the story of two sisters, Alice and Olive Barton, daughters of a Catholic landlord in Galway, as they return home on completing their convent education in England and negotiate the marriage market of the Dublin Season. There is a counterpoint between the girls: the beautiful but silly Olive, attracted to the 'unsuitable' Captain Hibbert but pushed by her mother into pursuit of title and money in the form of a match with Lord Kilcarney, and the clever, plainer sister Alice, who feels stifled by the emptiness of the life around her. Alice finally escapes to a more intellectually satisfying life as a writer in London, through marriage to a man her family considers beneath her, a doctor whose practical idealism matches her own. Set in 1882–3, the novel explores landlord attitudes and responses to the land war. Moore describes the bargaining over rent, landlord fears of venturing away from home in case of attack, and their concern about the future of their way of life. The setting and atmosphere of the novel were to be echoed in *Parnell and His Island*, although the essays are darker in tone.

As Brendan Fleming has pointed out, Moore employed the metaphor of Dublin Bay in the opening pages of *Parnell and His Island* as a mirror 'enabling perfect reflection of the present condition of Ireland and prediction of the country's future'.[15] The essays were originally intended to present Ireland and the land conflict to a French readership, a response to the lively interest with which events in Ireland were followed in France. They were written after *A Drama in Muslin* and revisit many of the themes touched upon in it—indeed, it may be seen as a companion piece to the novel.[16] However, *A Drama in Muslin* had been roundly denounced by reviewers, appalled by its feminism, its atheism and the openness of its treatment of unwed pregnancy, adultery and lesbianism, as well as its naturalistic style. But rather than restrain his pen in response, Moore seems to have been goaded into unleashing the full fury of his satire and transgressing the boundaries of Victorian taste and morality still further in *Parnell and His Island*. In February 1886, following the serialisation of *A Drama in Muslin*, which had commenced in January, he wrote to his mother: 'I am very sorry indeed I cannot go to Moore Hall this year. Nothing would give me greater pleasure than to spend a few months with you in the old place but I hear my book has given so much offence that it would be better for me to keep away.'[17] If his novel had offended his Irish relatives, publication of *Parnell and His Island* was a definitive burning of bridges. He was not to return to Moore Hall until the death of his mother in 1895.

As reflected in *Parnell and His Island*, Moore's attitude to his tenants and the land question was complex. In his childhood he had found them frightening and alien but on his return to Moore Hall in 1880 he came to a shocked realisation of the hardship of their lives. Letters to the *Freeman's Journal* and the *Mayo Examiner* in the autumn of 1880 urge agreement between landlords and tenants to propose a land bill that would offer relief in the crisis.[18] Like his father, George Henry Moore (1811–70), he was in favour of Home Rule and, in Adrian Frazier's words, 'bleakly supportive of Gladstone and Parnell'.[19]

But Moore also depicts the degeneration of the Land League from its early idealism into terrorism in the countryside and cynicism on the part of the leaders. In the penultimate scene of *A Drama in Muslin*, as Alice Barton and Dr Reed, her new husband, leave Galway, they come upon an eviction. Reed rescues the family by paying their rent, only to see the onlookers offering to show the eviction party the way to the next victim for the price of a drink. He exclaims:

And to think . . . that they are the same peasants that we once saw so firmly banded that it seemed as if nothing would ever again separate them, that nothing would ever again render them cowardly and untrue to each other; is it possible that those wretched hirelings, so ready to betray, so eager to lick the hand that smites them, are the same men whom we saw two years ago united by one thought, organised by one determination to resist the oppressor, marching firmly to nationhood?[20]

His disillusion seems to echo that of the author. Yet if Moore holds out little hope for the tenant side, he feels a deep sense of shame for his role as a landlord (see p. 3 below). The institution of landlordism in Ireland is indefensible and Moore, who accepts 'the socialist axiom that capital is only a surplus-value coming from unpaid labour', is well aware of its exploitative nature.[21] Indeed, his decision to make the land crisis a theme of *A Drama in Muslin* and *Parnell and His Island* may have arisen from a need to explore his own mixed emotions about the issue.

Ireland was much visited by travellers and commentators in the nineteenth century, the majority of whom would have started from Dublin, as did another absentee landlord, Lord Colambre in his investigation of his native land in Maria Edgeworth's novel, *The Absentee* (1812). Moore's narrative follows this pattern, the first chapters treating the capital and its society, after which the location moves westward to the countryside of his native Mayo. The opening chapter, after characterising Dublin as shabby, like 'an old clothes shop', and intellectually barren ('nobody reads and nobody thinks'), is divided into four parts that Moore see as representing the city: 'The Castle'; 'The Shelbourne Hotel'; 'The Kildare Street Club'; and the establishment of the dressmaker, 'Mrs. Rusville'. His points of focus are those of the Irish landed gentry, although he is also aware of the seamier side of the city, which he notes with an artist's eye for detail and the naturalist's relentless will to describe it.[22] Dublin Castle was the centre of the British administration in Ireland. As a member of the Catholic landed gentry and the son of an Irish Nationalist MP, his attitude to the Castle was ambivalent.[23] His background gave him entrée to the Castle and he took part in the Dublin 'Season' in 1883 and 1884, attending the Levée, the Drawing Rooms and Castle Balls.[24] He had not, however, been to a State Dinner and had the temerity to write to the chamberlain, Colonel Dease, to ask for an invitation, for the purposes of researching background for his novel. The Castle officials, not wishing to see their ceremonies exposed, tried to put him off and finally rejected the request. Moore then mischievously published the correspondence in the *Freeman's Journal*,[25] earning him the approval of Justin Huntly McCarthy, son of the Nationalist MP, Justin McCarthy. A writer and journalist like Moore, McCarthy wrote of how pleased he was 'at your battle with the Castle blunderers and at your very decided victory over the Prince of the power of the air', adding, 'I regard you as our best ally in our crusade against that stronghold of shame'.[26] In *Parnell and His Island*, Moore's approach is merciless, depicting the Viceroy's 'mock court', in which the girls presented, in a parallel ceremony to presentation to the Queen, submit to being kissed by the Lord Lieutenant, in a ceremony which Moore hints has unsavoury echoes of the *droit de seigneur*.[27] The girls 'brought out' for the Dublin season are described as 'muslin martyrs', exhibited in society with the sole intention of attracting husbands, also a central theme in *A Drama in Muslin*. Moore's sympathy for women is evident in much of his writing; many of the main characters of his novels are women struggling against the restrictions imposed on them by society.[28] Here he depicts the pitiless competition for dancing (and ultimately marriage) partners acted out in the ballroom, which 'for the majority is a place of torture and despair'.

The subject of the marriage race is continued in Moore's account of the Shelbourne Hotel, where many of the girls stay during the Dublin season.[29] In *Parnell and His Island*, the comfort of Dublin's premier hotel provides the setting for the frank discussion about marriage prospects taking place among the women. Just around the corner from the Shelbourne Hotel was the Kildare Street Club, 'one of the most impor-tant institutions in Ireland . . . a sort of oyster-bed into which all the eldest sons of the landed gentry fall as a matter of course'. He describes its denizens watching, open-mouthed, from the club's windows as a National League procession passes in the street. Mrs. Rusville, the fashionable dressmaker, appears in *A Drama in Muslin* as Mrs. Symonds, although in *Parnell and His Island* her establishment is portrayed in more lurid tones of drunkenness and scandalmongery, in line with the progression in Moore's negativity from *Drama* to *Parnell*. Like so many of her clients, she seeks an opportunity to launch her three daughters at a Vice-Regal ball. He was referring in his portrait to Mrs. Sims, the famous Dublin dressmaker, whom the Countess of Fingall described in her memoirs: 'The position of Worth in Paris could not have been more firmly established and more magnificent than that of Mrs. Sims in Dublin of those days. . . . She kept us in our places, and we were humble before her.'[30]

From Dublin, the scene shifts to a country house in Mayo, where Moore relates the circumstances of his host, a land-lord and land agent, who must endure life under constant armed guard to protect him against Land League assassins.[31] Nevertheless, he points out that despite the perceived dangers, 'the gentry in Mayo enjoy themselves very well indeed'. Several of the details of Moore's account were based on the homes of his relatives, the Blakes, O'Connors and Ruttledges, with whom he had stayed in 1880–4. It was somewhat disingenuous of him to claim in a letter to his mother that: 'I am more sorry than I can say that the Ruttledges are under the impression that I described Cornfield [the Ruttledges' home] in *The Figaro*: I never thought of doing any such thing.'[32] He had given the agent the same first name as Tom Ruttledge, whom he had appointed his own agent in 1880. Meanwhile his uncle's name, Blake, is given to his account of a landlord, who, after a prolonged affair with the daughter of one of his tenants, decides to marry for money and packs her and their five children off to America. He adds 'I know of no novelist who has touched this subject, and yet how full it is of poor human nature: vice, degradation, pity, hard-heartedness, grow on its every branch like blackberries in an autumn hedge.' The fact that the story was actually true makes Moore's indiscretion breathtaking.[33] While for the most part he blends, distorts and caricatures real individuals in *Parnell and His Island*, the book is sufficiently autobiographical to have invited attempts to identify characters in it. Moreover, he was sensitive enough to have known what effect these portrayals would have. Could it be that they were, to some degree at least, acts of revenge for a childhood in which he had been mocked by his parents and relatives as stupid and ugly?[34] Here was the ugly duckling returned as, if not a swan, at least a moderately successful, urbane author, whilst his re-engagement with his native land may have stirred memories of past humiliations.

'The House of an Irish Poet' is the most intriguing of these essays, in that in the account of a day trip to 'Lake Mount' (Moore Hall), Moore makes an appearance, not as the narrator but in the character of the Irish poet, the 'Landlord M——', newly returned from Paris. Here he shows a very keen understanding of how he must have appeared to others—odd in his French clothes, with his books of poetry, out of place and slightly absurd. But this was not the Moore of 1887 but himself in 1880. As Elizabeth Grubgeld points out, this portrayal is of his younger self. '. . . the explicit designation of "Landlord M——" as a poet identifies him with the author of *Flowers of Passion* (1878) and *Pagan Poems* (1881), while distinguishing him from the author who, by 1887, was known almost exclusively as a novelist.'[35] He reproduces an interview between M—— and his tenants which closely follows that between Arthur Barton and his tenants in *A Drama in Muslin*,[36] both of which were probably based on exchanges between Moore and his own tenants in 1880–1.

In 'The Tenant-Farmer' we see Moore expressing all the prejudice and class fear of the Irish landlord. If writers such as Yeats, Lady Gregory and, to a lesser extent, Synge, tended to idealise the Irish peasant, in their supposed lack of materialism, their spirituality and their strong ties to the soil,[37] Moore veers in the opposite direction. Micky Moran is compared in social-Darwinian terms to 'some low-earth animal whose nature has not yet risen from out the soil. He is evidently of a degenerate race—a race that has been left behind—and should perish, like the black rat perished before the brown and more ferocious species.' (p. 36 below) But instead of dying out, this race is making way against the 'superior races' owing to 'their extraordinary power of reproduction'. If Moore excoriated the landlords for their parasitic role, his description of the population of the West of Ireland, whom he identified as 'Fins', describing them as 'the most ill-favoured race that ever trod the earth' is extraordinarily racist. Nevertheless, he understands very well the tenant's terror of eviction and how the prospects of deterring landlords from evictions and winning rent reductions were powerful reasons for supporting both the Land League and engaging in agrarian violence. Despite his claims of being out of touch with his own affairs as a landed proprietor, Moore here shows himself to be fully conversant with the realities of the peasant economy, providing details of crop acreage and Moran's expected income from migrant labour in England. His account of Mary Moran and her seduction and banishment from her family's home demonstrates his concern for the outcast single mother, a theme to which he was to return in his most successful novel, *Esther Waters* (1894).

Miserably unhappy schooldays at the fashionable but harsh Catholic boarding school of Oscott left Moore with a deep hostility to Catholicism. In *Confessions of a Young Man*, he claimed 'Two dominant notes in my character—an original hatred of my native country, and a brutal loathing of the religion I was brought up in.'[38] In 1903 he converted to Anglicanism as a protest against Maynooth's reception of King Edward VII, but in fact he was a life-long atheist, having ceased to believe in God in his teens.[39] Catholicism as an institution was, however, a recurrent theme in several of his novels, including *The Lake*, *Evelyn Innes*, *Sister Teresa* and portions of his three-volume autobiography, *Hail and Farewell* (1911–14). In his treatment of Fr Tom Shannon, in the essay on 'The Priest' in *Parnell and His Island*, we see a man 'proud, ostentatious, overbearing' but, as Moore points out, of limited intelligence. He is well informed about politics but neither the covert Fenian of much of the pro-landlord writing about priests,[40] nor the saintly figure of many of the nationalist treatments.[41] In *Parnell and His Island*, Fr Shannon, the son of a grocer, steers a difficult course between landlords and tenants. He dislikes the Land League, especially its radical, violent following, yet he remains powerless to oppose it.[42]

James Daly, the leader of the local Land League branch, is the subject of the next essay, ironically entitled 'The Patriot'. Daly, the son of a bailiff who had been dismissed for stealing, insolence and drunkenness, becomes a cattle grazier and journalist, a founder of the Land League and is later elected as a Member of Parliament. Once in London, he finds himself seduced by the city and its comforts; his manners and tastes are refined as he 'frequents fashionable restaurants, sips champagne and chats fluently with actresses'. In one of the passages removed by the publisher of the English edition, Moore has Daly delighting in the clean body of the common London prostitute, since his previous sexual encounters were with beggar-women in a dirty field amid the cow-pats, outside the walls of the county town.[43] He will not return to the West of Ireland with its 'rank smells of the dung-heap, the pig, the damp cabin, the dirty paraffin-oil odour of the West' but make his way in London or America. Moore is once more being provocative, even libellous here, as there was a well-known James Daly, editor of the *Connaught Telegraph* and a founder of the Land League, who had also earned his living from cattle-grazing. While Daly declined to run for parliament, he was in the late 1870s what one historian has called 'the most influential man in Mayo'.[44] Grubgeld has suggested that the character of James Daly was based on a composite of the real James Daly and John O'Connor Power, MP for County Mayo and Daly's ally. She proposes that in rejecting the Daly/O'Connor type as unrefined, he may also have been trying to make a distinction between opportunist politicians such as these and the idealism of other nationalists, personified by Michael Davitt. Several months prior to Moore's visit to Ireland in 1880–1, a breach between Davitt and O'Connor Power had become public and would have been widely discussed in Mayo and elsewhere.[45] However, while individuals like the Daly portrayed by Moore may have existed among Irish Party members, his portrait in *Parnell and His Island* was an unjust slur on the characters of both the real Daly and John O'Connor Power, neither of whom resembled the nonentity he depicts. Daly and O'Connor Power differed with Parnell and his followers on issues of principle—most notably in their claims that the interests of small farmers of the West were being overlooked by the land movement and in resisting the centralising tendencies of the parliamentarians.[46] Like Moore's Daly, O'Connor Power was unable to resist the lure of upper-class London society, while in Tim Healy's words, he 'reeked of the common clay'.[47] Healy relates that 'Parnell's aristocratic sensitiveness recoiled' in Power's presence but he was a strong enough figure to pose a real challenge to Parnell's leadership.[48] Moore's understanding of Irish politics was much less sure than his grasp of Irish society. In 1880, a leader in Daly's paper, *The Connaught Telegraph*, in announcing the appointment of Tom Ruttledge as Moore's new agent had described him as 'the degenerate son of a worthy father'.[49] Perhaps there was an element of settling old scores in his veiled attack on its editor.

'A Castle of Yesterday' introduces a hint of Gothic horror into Moore's narrative. While duck shooting on Lough Carra in the early morning, the author and his friend Dacre come ashore by Castle Carra. Sheltering in the ruins, the narrator begins to fantasise about its inhabitants centuries earlier, 'strong days that were better and happier than ours'. He is startled by a strange sound and ghostly shape that he takes for the 'white spirit of death'. 'The stair descends to an embrasure in the wall, and the moonlight is streaming through, and there is something there—a soft low snoring in the moonlight; the staircase descends before me, but I cannot follow it, I cannot pass this ghostly ray of moonlight.' (p. 63) It is in fact a snowy owl, which Dacre shoots by mistake on leaving the castle. However, Brendan Fleming has suggested that the scene may be read as a metaphor for the threat posed to landlords such as Moore by 'Captain Moonlight', the popular term applied to agrarian crime. 'The attempt to seek escape into a nostalgia for a time preceding the land agitation is undone by the omnipresent moonlight.'[50]

From the ruined Castle Carra, 'A Castle of Yesterday' or in the French edition 'Un chateau mort', Moore moves to describe, in 'A Castle of To-Day' a visit to Ashford Castle, the neo-Gothic home of Lord and Lady Ardilaun at Cong. Moore exclaims over the beauty of the setting, remarking that 'after a week spent in the thin, mean poverty of the north-west, amid the sadness of ruined things, this strangely beautiful castle renders me singularly happy'. Lady Ardilaun, herself a painter, was interested in what Moore could tell her about the new artistic movements in France and they were to enjoy a long friendship. During Moore's visit Lord Ardilaun, the Guinness magnate, was having a moat constructed to protect him against possible attack by dynamiters. He is unpopular, Moore is told, partly because he is wealthy enough to resist the Land League, and also because he is a Protestant and a Conservative. There is an element of snobbery in Moore's

relish of his visit but his admiration for Ardilaun's philanthropy is sincere.[51] In the 1890s Moore was friendly with the
group of reformers around Horace Plunkett who attempted to
improve conditions in the countryside—work that became
known as 'constructive unionism', recognising the practical
value of their efforts (if at times lampooning them).[52]

The elegance and enchantment of Ashford Castle contrast
starkly with the images that follow in 'The Eviction'. Eviction
scenes were a common feature of novels of the period dealing
with the land question.[53] Moore's contemporary, J. M. Synge,
with similarly complex attitudes concerning his own landlord
background, wrote movingly about the distress caused by
evictions on Inis Mhean in *The Aran Islands* (1901). Moore had
included an eviction in *A Drama in Muslin*[54] but his treatment
in *Parnell and His Island* is striking in its relentless attention to
sordid detail. The brutality of the scenes, in which the pitiless
and drunken landlord Miss Barrett and her companion Miss
McCoy revel in the expulsion of the tenants from their homes,
were intended to shock. It is possible that the author's focus
on a female landlord was intended to deepen the horror,
given the assumptions about women current at the time.

It is in this chapter that the influence of Zola and the
naturalist school is most evident. In turn, Moore's essays may
have influenced Zola's writing of *La Terre*, and Joris-Karl
Huysmans' novel, *En Rade*. Zola had read and complimented
Moore on the publication of the essays in *Le Figaro* at a time
when he was engaged in writing *La Terre*. In a letter dated 15
August 1886, he wrote to Moore that his articles

pleased me immensely and I think they will have a real success.
Since I began reading them, an idea haunts me. Why not write
immediately a novel on Ireland? A social novel, alive, audacious,
revolutionary, which would be the life of liberty? England would be
in an uproar. Never has such an opportunity presented itself for the
shaking of a nation. Think of it. 'De l'audace, de l'audace, et encore
de l'audace.' [55]

In a sense, Moore had already tried to achieve such a social novel in *A Drama in Muslin*, although it is unclear whether Zola ever read it. Like Moore's work, Huysmans' *En Rade* included a snowy owl, feared by a fantasising nostalgic city man. However, Moore's 'Lettres sur l'Irlande' were serialised in *Le Figaro* several months before *En Rade* appeared in serialisation in *Revue indépendente*. [56]

If evictions contributed to the bitterness of the Land War, one response by tenants was through collective action in 'stopping the hunt'.[57] Hunting was a favourite pastime of the gentry and its prevention an effective means of challenging their authority. Tenants might refuse to give permission for the hunt to cross their land, or large crowds would gather in the area where the hunt was due to begin, frightening away any foxes or hares in the vicinity. Moore here also has the tenants stoning the hounds and perhaps poisoning the coverts. The conversation about Mrs. Jack and her niece Maggie seems to be another instance of Moore settling old scores (see pp. 82–4 below). Early in 1884 he had stayed with cousins, the Brownes at Brownes Grove near Tuam, County Galway. There he met and courted his cousin, Miss Maud Browne, and is thought to have proposed to her but been rejected. Like Maggie in *Parnell and His Island*, Maud was an heiress and would have married him but the aunt in whose care she was staying disapproved of him and prevented the match. He wrote to his mother:

I consider everything now over between me and Maud but I shall never forget the horrible system of terrorism to which she has been subjected. The poor girl's life is one of those unknown tragedies which the historian must pass without noticing but in which the histories of nations is written in as much as in the chronicle of battles and conquests.

But enough of the subject. Let the past be the past.[58]

Moore succeeded instead in transmuting her sad situation into art. In *A Drama in Muslin* she makes a brief appearance as the 'pale little martyr' at the State ball, 'who has spoken to no one, who has not even a brother to take her for a walk down the room, or to the buffet for an ice'.[59] In *Parnell and His Island* she is portrayed as Maggie Jordan, the object of pitying gossip, with whom Mr. Fleming, one of the hunting party, is encouraged to flirt in order to enrage her tyrannical aunt.

Moore's 'Conclusion' is the angriest part of an angry book and foreshadowed the renewal of the land war in the form of the Plan of Campaign, launched in October 1886.[60] There is a claim to artistic detachment in the opening paragraph: 'Unconcerned with this or that interest, indifferent to this or that opinion, my desire was to produce a series of pictures to touch the fancy of the reader as a Japanese ivory or fan, combinations of hue and colour calculated to awake in him fictitious feelings of pity, pitiful curiosity and nostalgia of the unknown.' (p. 89 below)

However, following his assertion that 'Ireland is a bog, and the aborigines (the Fins) are a degenerate race—short, squat, little men—with low foreheads and wide jaws', he launches into a detailed attack on what he calls 'the Parnell *régime*'. Whatever the tenant gained in reduced rents has been squandered in contributions to the Land League, idleness, drink and the frivolities of 'dreadful hats with ostrich feathers and shapeless mantles, and tea and eggs for breakfast'.[61] He sees Home Rule as inevitable but is far from sanguine about its effects. Of Parnell himself he says very little. His name crops up half a dozen times in the book, where he is a powerful presence offstage, a manipulator of events and men.[62] But it is striking that there is no discussion of Parnell in *Parnell and His Island*, apart from the assertion that: 'Of Parnell's leadership, it is unnecessary to say a word—the world knows of it; of the ability and courage of some dozen or twenty men grouped around him, I can speak with confidence—some of them are friends of mine, others I know through their writings. The rest of the party is composed of Mr. Dalys, music-hall managers, and publicans from Liverpool and Manchester,' who spend their time proving their patriotism by abusing the

landlords and condoning murder and outrage. (pp. 94–5)
Moore's attitude here is expressive not so much of artistic
detachment as passionate denunciation of Parnellism and its
effects. Yet, in Grubgeld's words: 'To judge Ireland with the
anger of *Parnell* is to reveal one's continuing relation to it,
especially when the judgements are coloured by a sense of
culpability.'[63] Moore was too close to, too formed by, the
society he described to attain the detachment he claimed.

Moore's re-engagement with Ireland in the early 1880s
had convinced him that he did not want to be an Irishman and
from then on his writing is characterised by what Grubgeld
terms his 'schizophrenia of citizenship' as a 'self-proclaimed
Irishman-turned-Frenchman-turned Englishman'.[64] As Adrian
Frazier has pointed out in his biography, he 'had no clear
affiliation with any single national tradition'. In England, he
was regarded as too sexy and French, whereas in Ireland he
was too French or too English.[65] As by nature something of an
outsider, it was easy to be an Irishman in Paris, far more
difficult to be an Irishman in Ireland. 'All the aspects of my
native country are violently disagreeable to me, and I cannot
think of the place I was born in without a sensation akin to
nausea.'[66] *Parnell and His Island* details his rejection of his
native land. Nevertheless, as Susan Mitchell observed: 'And if
one had no other evidence of his Irish origin, *Parnell and His
Island*, written with all the malignity of kinship, would have
revealed it.'[67]

The response to Moore's portrayal of Ireland was pre-
dictably hostile. The *Freeman's Journal* described his letters in
Le Figaro as 'extravagant caricatures; his assertions are often
infamous libels', although it allowed that 'there is truth and
power in the few sentences that paint the land system and tell
of its effects'.[68] *The Westminster Review* claimed that Moore
'presents facts or fictions as typical which are not so; and gives
everything warped and thrown out of position, as in a cheap
looking-glass'.[69] A reviewer in *The Academy* dismissed *Terre
d'Irlande* with the words 'as superficial in point of view as the
style is "gaulois"', and added: 'we should not be disposed to

anticipate for it a very favourable reception, if it is destined to be re-translated into English',[70] while a longer review in the 'Paris Day by Day' column of the London *Daily Telegraph* predicted: 'To say that Mr. Moore's exposure of his countrymen and countrywomen will provoke a storm of wrath against him would be superfluous'.[71] The only praise came from Moore's friend Mary Robinson, who described the book as 'a direct and truthful impression . . . clever, subtle, brutal, veracious'.[72] That there was not more of an outcry is probably due to the timing of the publication in June 1887, which coincided with the celebration of the Queen's Jubilee in Britain and the climax of the Plan of Campaign in the Bodyke evictions in Ireland.[73] Despite his protests, the circulating libraries banned it from their shelves.[74]

Parnell and His Island was one of a series of literary works that dealt with the land conflict. Indeed, literature became a weapon in a propaganda war between the sides, often seeking to explain the subject to a British readership.[75] Moore's work is unique, however, in that rather than taking sides he reviles both. Landlords are denounced for living off the poverty of their tenants, for which they contribute nothing in return. The system that maintains them is moribund and evictions are portrayed in all their brutal detail. But on the other hand, the tenants are repeatedly referred to in animalistic terms, reminiscent of the racist images of *Punch* magazine. Yet Moore was not a hostile outsider but the Irish son of a respected nationalist MP. *Parnell and His Island* was particularly damaging in a context in which nationalist writers were attempting to reposition the image of the Irish in more positive terms, as noble, patriotic, genteel, and above all moral.[76]

Moore's transgression was not forgotten. Over a decade later, when he became active in the Irish Literary Society, complaints were made to W. B. Yeats for having introduced the author of *Parnell and his Island* and of *A Drama in Muslin* into a patriotic movement.[77] Yeats and Edward Martyn had the difficult task of pacifying his critics to enable Moore to make what was to be an important contribution to the early development of the Abbey Theatre. In *Salve*, volume 2 of his memoir *Hail and Farewell*, Moore relates a conversation with Douglas Hyde who warns him that 'Your book *Parnell and His Island* will go against you with the [Gaelic] League.' Moore has him suggest that the League might be reconciled to it if he were to reissue it as *Parnell and His Island, or Ireland Without Her Language*.[78] By 1916 Susan Mitchell found it 'indecent in the revolting display he [Moore] makes of his country's hurt' and accused him of 'exhibiting his country's sores for the coppers of the Paris press',[79] Moore himself later dismissed it as 'mere gabble' and wished it banished into oblivion. In 1921 he listed it as one of his works which 'if they are ever printed again, should be issued as the work of a disciple—Amico Moorini I put forward as a suggestion'.[80]

Nevertheless, *Parnell and His Island* should not be dismissed so lightly by readers today. As a pioneering work of naturalist writing on Ireland, it is important in terms of literary history. In its echoes and elaborations of similar themes, it may also be read as a companion work to *A Drama in Muslin*, one of the outstanding Irish novels of the late nineteenth century. If there are excesses, there are also beautifully written passages and many of its images are powerful and memorable. *Parnell and His Island* is an important historical document. However jaundiced a view Moore takes, he knew his subject well and he gives us a more complex and nuanced account of the realities and attitudes of Ireland in the 1880s than most authors of his day. He is as perceptive in describing the manners and behaviour of his own class as in portraying the fears and resentments of the tenant, Mickey Moran. He refuses to paint in black and white, expressing his sympathy for Captain Boycott, 'my friend and neighbour' and for Lord Ardilaun, while at the same time the institution of landlordism is denounced in no uncertain terms. And for all his merciless portrayal of 'the patriot', he salutes the strength of patriotic feeling held by James Daly and his associates (see p. 56 below). His more layered portrayal of the Ireland of his day has a greater appeal today than it did for a society torn by the partisanship of battle. *Parnell and His Island* bears out George W. Russell's perceptive comment about Moore in his obituary in 1933, where he described him as 'One of the most talented and unfilial of Ireland's children . . . he loved the land even if he did not love the nation'.[81]

ACKNOWLEDGEMENTS.

I should like to acknowledge the role of Barbara Mennell throughout the preparation of this book, whose assistance extended far beyond the normal contribution of an editor and whose enthusiasm was much appreciated. W. J. Mc Cormack generously lent both his copy of *Parnell and His Island* and his literary expertise in commenting on the Introduction. Margaret Kelleher and my father, Justin Keating, also read the Introduction and made invaluable suggestions for revisions. Alan English kindly checked and corrected my translations of French passages from *Terre d'Irlande* and James H. Murphy provided assistance with a reference. The responsibility for any remaining errors is mine.

The National Gallery is gratefully thanked for permission to reproduce John Yeats's portrait of George Moore on the cover of this book. The staff of the National Library of Ireland and of the Library of St Patrick's College were very helpful. I must thank my colleagues at the Department of History, St Patrick's College, Drumcondra, for their support and for providing such a pleasant environment in which to work. My parents Justin Keating and Laura Kleanthous have, as always, been a source of inspiration and encouragement. My son, Jonah, patiently put up with all my talk about George Moore.

Carla King
St Patrick's College, Drumcondra
February 2004

A NOTE ON THE TEXT.

The essays in this collection first appeared separately under the title 'Lettres sur l'Irlande' as a series of six weekly articles in *Le Figaro*, 31 July to 4 September 1886. They were published in volume form in French with some additions, as *Terre d'Irlande*, translated into French by M. F. Rabbé and published by G. Charpentier & Co., Paris, in 1887. The first edition of *Parnell and His Island* was published by Swan Sonnenschein, Lowrey & Co. London, in 1887, with deletions made by Herbert Wigram, editor of the publishing house. The text used in the preparation of the present publication is that of the first edition. However, in order to restore the integrity of Moore's original text, the passages removed by Wigram from *Terre d'Irlande* are included in the notes in the original French, followed by translations. Passages which are included in *Parnell and His Island* but omitted from *Terre d'Irlande* are also indicated in the notes.

PARNELL AND HIS ISLAND.

This is Dalkey, a suburb of Dublin. From where I stand I look down upon the sea as on a cup of blue water; it lies two hundred feet below me like a great smooth mirror; it lies beneath the blue sky as calm, as mysteriously still, as an enchanted glass in which we may read the secrets of the future.[1] How perfectly cuplike is the bay! Blue mountains, blue embaying mountains, rise on every side, and amorously the sea rises up to the lip of the land. These mountains of the north, these Turner-like mountains, with their innumerable aspects, hazy perspectives lost in delicate grey, large and trenchant masses standing out brutally in the strength of the sun, are as the mailed arms of a knight leaning to a floating siren whose flight he would detain and of whom he asks still an hour of love.[2] I hear the liquid murmur of the sea; it sings to the shore as softly as a turtle-dove to its mate. I see white sails scattered over the grey backgrounds of the sky, and through the dissolving horizon other sails appear and disappear, lighter than the large wings of the sea-gull that floats and plunges, sometimes within a few feet of the cliff's edge, a moment after there are a hundred feet between it and the sea. My thoughts turn involuntarily to the Bay of Naples, which I have never seen, but perfect though it be—Nature's fullest delight above which no desire may soar—it cannot be more beautiful than the scene which now lies blue and translucid before me.

I am two hundred feet above a sea striped with purple and violet; and above my head the rocks rise precipitously. From every side the mountains press with voluptuous arms the voluptuous sea: above my head the villas are perched like birds amid the rocks. There I see a bouquet of trees, here I see a green sward where the white dresses of the young girls playing tennis float this way and that. From villa to villa a white road winds, like a thread leading through the secrets of a labyrinth; sometimes it is lost in a rocky entanglement, sometimes it vanishes in the dark and long shadows of a pine wood; sometimes it is suspended, it is impossible to say how, out of the mountain-side, and higher still spread out on the clear sky, and crowning the mountain-brow is the imperial heather.

In the exquisite clarity of the day every detail is visible; and as my glance passes from the highest heights down to the depths of the shore I see women in long bathing-dresses crawling up the strand far away: they appear like flies: the naked flesh of some boys bathing shines in the sun ray, they are climbing up the black sides of a boat,—that one on the prow joins his hands above his head and disappears in the purple of the waves.[3] On the terrace by me stands a fat man, the type of commercial prosperity (he is a distiller); his family is about him, enjoying the delicate listlessness of this summer afternoon. Now I hear the rushing rumble of a train, the strident whistle tears the air and is repeated high and far through the sonorous distances of this strange mountain. The eye follows the white steam across the bridge; then the train is lost in a tunnel; now it re-appears and turning and twisting it scuttles away like a rabbit through the rocks.

No town in the world has more beautiful surroundings than Dublin. Seeing Dalkey one dreams of Monte Carlo, or better still of the hanging gardens of Babylon, of marble balustrades, of white fountains, of innumerable yachts, of courts of love, and of sumptuous pleasure places; but alas, all that meets the eye are some broken-down villas! The white walls shine in the sun and deceive you, but if you approach you will find a front-door where the paint is peeling, and a ruined garden.

And in such ruin life languishes here! The inhabitants of the villas are, for the most part, landlords whom circumstances have forced to shut up their houses and to come here to economise; or, they may belong to the second class of land-lords: widows living on jointures paid by the eldest sons, or mortgagees upon money placed by them or by their ancestors upon the land. For in Ireland there is nothing but the land; with the exception of a few distillers and brewers in Dublin, who live upon the drunkenness of the people, there is no way in Ireland of getting money except through the peasant.

The socialistic axiom that capital is only a surplus-value coming from unpaid labour, either in the past or in the present, is in other countries mitigated and lost sight of in the multiplicity of ways through which money passes before falling into the pockets of the rich; but in Ireland the passage direct and brutal of money from the horny hands of the peasant to the delicate hands of the proprietor is terribly suggestive of serfdom.[4] In England the landlord lays out the farm and builds the farm-buildings. In Ireland he does absolutely nothing. He gives the bare land to the peasant, and sends his agent to collect the half-yearly rent; in a word he allows the peasant to keep him in ease and luxury. 'I am an Irish land-lord, I have done this, I do this, and I shall continue to do this, for it is as impossible for me as for the rest of my class to do otherwise; but that doesn't prevent me from recognising the fact that it is a worn-out system, no longer possible in the nineteenth century, and one whose end is nigh.'[5] In Ireland every chicken eaten, every glass of champagne drunk, every silk dress trailed in the street, every rose worn at a ball, comes straight out of the peasant's cabin. A few years ago this tribute (for in Ireland rent is a tribute and nothing else) was accepted without astonishment, without an after-thought, absolutely—as in other ages the world accepted slavery and feudalism.

But one day, suddenly, without warning, the scales fell from the eyes of the people, and the people resolved to rid themselves of this plague.[6] Visible hitherto only to a small number, and they denied its existence save in the poorest districts, this plague-spot is apparent to-day to every eye; it is visible everywhere, even in the heart of the slums as in the most elegant suburb; it was as if a veil had been drawn revealing the boils with which the flesh of Ireland is covered.

You see that coarse, common man dressed in a greasy, worn-out tweed jacket, smoking a black pipe at the end of the weed-grown terrace of the dilapidated villa which he has hired for the season? He is speaking to his daughter, a sad-looking girl dressed in a long red cashmere buttoned down the back; she tells him that she wants a new dress to go to a tennis party in the neighbourhood. He grumbles, he thinks she had better not accept any more tennis parties this year. Does he want her to remain an old maid? Nothing is done for her that she may get a husband; no parties are given for her, never is there a young man invited to the house. Finally he draws from his pocket a roll of bank-notes black and greasy, notes with worn-out edges, notes cut in two and stuck together, notes which smell of the smoke of the cabin, notes that are rancid of the sweat of the fields, notes which have been spat upon at fairs for good luck, notes which are an epitome of the sufferings of the peasant in the west of Ireland.

The young girl runs away skipping with three or four of these notes to buy a dress, to dream of the husband which she will never get; the man sinks into gloom, dreaming of the Land League and of the possibility of getting out of the tenants in the autumn what they refused to pay in the spring;[7] and I dreaming of the bank-notes, of the husband-hunting girl, of the ruined proprietor, of the villa in ruins. I read in all this, as in an epitaph upon a tomb, the history of a vanished civilisation. Then as my thoughts return to the beautiful landscape— with its broken rocks full of lights and shades, its bits of white road and the strange railway suspended as if by magic above the blue bay, and the violet mountains standing out against the silver clouds, I dream of Paris and of what Paris would be if within a few miles of so beautiful a panorama. Paris would sing in this bay; Paris would dance on these terraces; columns and palaces, balustrades, arches and cupolas would extend from height to height the enchantment of their architecture. The calm and sombre waters of the bay, illuminated by gondolas coming and gondolas going—white beneath the moon, yellow and gold beneath the lamps—would be a floating dream; fireworks darting from the abrupt hollows of the dark hill-side, would jewel the forehead of the night, detonations of champagne, cries of the dancers, blaring of the *cors de chasse* and the sonorous mountain echoing with the various sounds of festival.

And still dreaming of my Irish France I listened to the monotonous cry of a broken barrel-organ, and, looking at the poor devil of an Italian, I know well that nobody here, except perhaps the distiller, is rich enough to throw him a penny.

Far away those are the Wicklow mountains. Bound about Dublin like a blue scarf, they are as bright notes of joy in the pale monotony of the pale dim streets.

The character of Dublin is the absence of any characteristic touch. Dublin is neither ugly, nor pretty, nor modern, nor ancient, but all these qualifications might be applied to it as to an 'old-clo' shop.' Yes, Dublin reminds me of an old-clothes shop where ball-dresses, dress coats, morning trowsers, riding habits, wellington boots, lace shawls are to be let or sold. Nothing seems really to belong to anyone. Everybody might have owned everything—language, dress, and manners—at one time or another. The streets are built of pale brown bricks, a pale poor brown—poor but honest. Nor are they built at hazard, improvised like London streets, but set out artificially in squares and monotonous lines, like a town that a tired child might have improvised out of a box of bricks. Here you find no architectural surprises, like in other towns; no alleys or curious courts filled with life—strange, picturesque, and enigmatic; none of those singular byways with reft of sky in the brick entanglement, sometimes bulging out into courts; where shops of fried fish, coal shops, shops of old iron and old paper, lean one against the other in giddy confusion; sometimes slipping into passages narrow and twisted, where bands of little children dance joyously to the sound of a friendly organ.[8]

'We are poor but honest,' the houses cry aloud, and in their faded elegance they bend and bow like ladies who have seen better times. Others who would give themselves fashionable airs trail their finery like a middle-aged coquette in a provincial town. The flower-boxes rot in the windows, the rose-coloured window-blinds are torn, the railings rot with rust, the areas exhale the fœtid odours of un-emptied dust-bins;[9] add to this the noise of a hundred pianos; imagine a society of ill-bred young girls, making love to a few briefless barristers, their clerks, the employés in the breweries; beat this all up to waltz music from four o'clock in the afternoon till four in the morning, with an interval of three hours or so for dinner, and you will have realised the exterior aspect of Dublin society.

The following conversation which I overheard in 'the best society,' will give an idea of the general culture and the normal *esprit* of Dublin girls.

Scene, a ball-room. Dramatis personæ, two officers and a charming girl. First officer: 'By Jove, what a pretty girl you have been dancing with! She is really a Juno, she is superb. You must introduce me to her.'

Second officer: 'She is not ugly, but I don't think you would care about her, she's rather common.'

'Common with that face, impossible!'

The two men approach the beauty. He who thinks her common leaves her with him who considers her divine. I listen to see how this acquaintance, so happily begun, will end. Overcome with emotion the lover seeks for words; should he begin by speaking of the weather, or of the excellence of the floor? Important question! At last the young girl breaks silence, and whilst her admirer is still seeking for a transitional phase to lead up to more important matter, she says, after having examined him from head to foot: 'Ah Captain, what a little foot you've got!'

In the sombre and sad streets of Dublin there are two open spaces—Stephen's Green and Merrion Square. The first—which has lately been reclaimed from its Indian-jungle-like state and decorated with mounds and bridges and ponds, and presented to the city by a rich nobleman[10]—resembles in its present state a school-treat for charity children; the other still flourishes in all its ancient dilapidation;[11] rusty iron railings, decrepit trees, and a few lamentable tennis players; in the deep ruts of the roads two or three outside cars lie hidden—that singular vehicle which defies description, two wheels with seats suspended on either side and from which you will certainly be thrown if you don't hold on with all your might.[12]

On every door in Merrion Square there is a brass plate. For there are more doctors and lawyers in Dublin than any other city in the world. Dublin is a town of officials. Every man wears the red ribbon of the Castle[13] in his button-hole; and more than one woman wears it instead of a garter.

Nobody reads, nobody thinks. To be considered a man of the world, it is only necessary to have seen one or two plays in London before they are six months old, and to curse the Land League. In the 'best society' I have met with young men who have never read 'Vanity Fair'[14] and young women who have never heard of Leonardo da Vinci.[15] Once I was dining with a Mr. Ryan; on the club[16] table there were two photographs, one was of Richard Wagner and the other was of Beethoven.

Mr. Ryan: 'Who is that?'

I: 'That is Wagner.'[17]

Mr. Ryan: 'Who is Wagner?'

I (recovering myself with an effort): 'Don't you know? Richard Wagner, the great breeder of shorthorns!'

Mr. Ryan: 'Begorra 'tis strange I niver came across him in Ballinasloe; and who is the other?'

I: 'That is Beethoven.'

Mr. Ryan: 'Who is Beethoven?'

I: 'Don't you know? He is the great breeder of cobs.'

Mr. Ryan: 'And I niver met him at the Dublin horse show; does he niver go there? Tell me—are you listening to me?—what sort of stock does he go in for?'

Dublin is in a barbarous state, and, what is worse, in a retrograde state.

. . . . .

Dublin is divided into four parts: The Castle, the Shelbourne Hotel, the Kildare Street Club, and Mrs. Rusville the fashionable dressmaker.

THE CASTLE.

To describe the Castle it is only necessary to compare it to an immense police barrack. It is devoid of all architecture, and the brick walls are as bare and as bald as an official document; everything, even to the red coats of the sentinels, reminds you of the red tape with which these documents are tied.[18] The Castle rises like a upas tree amid ruins and death; the filth of the surrounding streets is extreme. The Castle dominates the Liffey—a horrible canal or river flowing between two stone embankments. Curious and characteristic details: between the bridges great sea-gulls fly back and forwards with a mechanical regularity, diving from time to time after the rubbish which the current bears away to the sea.

On either side there are sombre and sinister streets, aged and decrepit buildings filled with old books rotting in dark and fœtid confusion; dark holes where, in Rembrandt *chiaroscuro*, you see the form of a hag groping amidst heaps of something—something that may be clothes; shops where suspicious-looking women pretend to sell cheap cigars; others where placards announce the excellence of obscene goods manufactured on the premises; then the perspective floats in a slight curve, and is lost in the smoke of breweries and distilleries, an appropriate horizon for this town of miserable vice and hideous decrepitude.[19]

From the Castle the law in Ireland is administered, and it is there that the Viceroy[20] holds his mock Court; every sort of religious ceremony may be turned into ridicule, but it is certain, when a man not a king is forced to mimic royalty as far as possible, that everything that is grotesque in the original becomes in the imitation a caricature. The Viceroy is not an actor who consents to play a part, not a Messiah audacious enough to declare himself God, but something indefinable between the two that says: 'Of course you know that I am not a king, but I hope you will consider me one, and you will address me as such.' Such an anomaly necessitates a multitude of situations which are very suggestive of a Palais Royal farce. Although the Viceroy plays the part of a king, his wife is not authorised to play that of a queen.

How, therefore, is a drawing-room to be held? It is clear that the ladies who are presented cannot kiss the hand of the Viceroy as they kiss the hand of the Queen in Buckingham Palace.[21] A difficult situation of which this is the solution: the Viceroy must kiss the ladies. It is impossible to imagine anything more absurd than this Viceroy, an English nobleman, chosen for the post by the Government actually in power, standing upon a daïs surrounded by red guardsmen, all the ladies of the household behind him upon an estrade, kissing an interminable procession of women, young and old, fat and thin, as they are announced by the Chamberlain who reads out their names like a Doge's secretary in an opera bouffe.[22]

And then how are all the innumerable sinecures of the castle disposed of? Underlings, hirelings, of all sorts, swarm about this mock Court like flies about a putrefying carcass.[23] A sight indeed it is to see them marching in procession through the drawing-rooms after the presentations. The A.D.C.'s,[24] the Medical Department, the Private Secretary, the Military Private Secretary, the Assistant Under-Secretary, the Gentleman-in-Waiting, the Master of the Horse, the Dean of the Chapel Royal, the Chamberlain, the Gentlemen Ushers, the Controller, the State Steward walking with a wand, etc.[25] . . . It is easy, therefore, to understand the hatred of the people for the corruptions and injustices of the Castle.

The Castle is for the National party—to employ a comparison whose success is unquestionable—what a red flag is for a bull. This mock Court is considered as an absurdity by all classes of society except fashionable women to whom the fêtes of the Castle are of all importance. There are no mothers in Ireland as there are in France; it is not in the circle of their friends that they search for possible husbands for their daughters. As soon as a young girl has left school she is taken to Dublin, kissed by the Lord-Lieutenant, and let loose of the ball-rooms of the Castle to flirt as extravagantly or as discreetly as she thinks proper. In France the chaperon has a meaning; in England and Ireland she is a nonentity: from the moment a chaperon enters the ball-room till the time she leaves it she sees nothing of her charges. Still, nevertheless, the young girl passes four or five hours dancing; or, when an occasion presents itself, searches for a favourite corner hidden at the end of a dark corridor. The young girls without any great moral conscience make their way at the Castle, and those who are well introduced may amuse themselves, but for the majority it is a place of torture and despair. The girls outnumber the men in proportion of three to one, the competition is consequently severe; and it is pitiable to see these poor muslin martyrs standing at the door, their eyes liquid with invitation, striving to inveigle, to stay the steps of the men as they pass by. But although these balls are little else for the young girls than a series of heart-breaks, nevertheless the most abject basenesses are committed to secure an invitation.[26]

THE SHELBOURNE HOTEL.

The Shelbourne is a large and commodious hotel.[27] On entering, a winter garden on the first floor strikes a pleasant note of green, and a little fountain murmurs pleasantly amid grey stone frogs. The pen of Balzac would be necessary to describe the Shelbourne Hotel; it is the *pension* of Madame Vauquier[28] placed in aristocratic circles. For three pounds a week[29] you can live there; and this liberality on the part of the proprietor is singularly appreciated by widows and old maids of all sorts. The ladies' drawing-room is on the right, and Flaubert's celebrated phrase may be applied to it, 'It was the moral centre of the house.'[30] The walls are decorated with Swiss landscapes—mountains, chamois, cascades, and lakes. About the chimney-piece there are a great number of low chairs, chairs for invalid ladies, chairs made for novel reading

and for wool-work. Nothing is spoken of but men and marriages; it is here that all the scandals of Dublin are laid and
are hatched.

At this moment the drawing-room wears its most habitual
air. Two old ladies are seated on the sofa knitting. Two old
maids who come up every year husband-hunting, are sitting
artlessly advancing their little slippered feet; between them is
the chaperon who has brought them to Dublin for the Castle
season.

'Oh, so you have all come up to the Castle, and are going
to be presented![31] Well, you'll find the rooms very grand and
the suppers very good, and if you know a lot of people,
particularly the officers quartered here, you will find the
Castle balls very amusing. The best way to do is to come to
town a month before the drawing-room and give a ball; and
in that way you get to know all the men. If you haven't done
that I'm afraid you won't get many partners. Even if you do
get introduced they will only ask you to dance, and you will
never see them again. Dublin is like a race-course, men come
and speak to you and pass on. It is pleasant enough if you
know people, but as for marriages there are none, I assure
you. I know lots of girls, and very nice girls too, who have
been going up for six or seven years, and have not been able
to pull it off.'

'And ah,' said a girl speaking with a terrible brogue, 'the
worst of it is that the stock is for iver increasing; ivery year we
are growing more and more numerous, and the men seem to
be getting fewer. Nowadays a man won't look at you unless
you have at least two thousand[32] a year.'

At the Shelbourne the fashionable world stays during the
Castle season. The hotel is then as full of girls as a beehive of
bees; their clear voices are heard in the corridors, and the
staircase is gay with passing and rustling silk; and then, too, is
made manifest the morality which is so characteristic of all
English-speaking countries where young girls have acquired
the same liberty as men. Complete freedom of speech is
granted them.[33] In Dublin a virgin is scarcely a favourable

specimen of virginity: scandals, divorce cases, and invitations to the Castle are the sole themes of her conversation.

THE KILDARE STREET CLUB.

The Kildare Street Club is one of the most important institutions in Dublin.[34] It represents in the most complete acceptation of the word the rent party in Ireland; better still, it represents all that is respectable, that is to say, those who are gifted with an oyster-like capacity for understanding this one thing: that they should continue to get fat in the bed in which they were born.[35] This club is a sort of oyster-bed into which all the eldest sons of the landed gentry fall as a matter of course. There they remain spending their days, drinking sherry and cursing Gladstone[36] in a sort of dialect, a dead language which the larva-like stupidity of the club has preserved. The green banners of the League are passing,[37] the cries of a new Ireland awaken the dormant air, the oysters rush to their window—they stand there open-mouthed, real pantomime oysters, and from the corner of Frederick Street a group of young girls[38] watch them in silent admiration.

MRS. RUSVILLE.[39]

To this sympathetic dressmaker all fashionable figures are confided, and all highbred griefs and scandals.

When the giggling countess leaves, the sighing marchioness is received with genial sympathy.

'My dear Helen, I can bear up no longer; my husband is a brute! It is only here I find any comfort; you only are kind.' Overcome with emotion the women fall into each other's arms and they kiss fervently. Finally, they retire to Mrs. Rusville's boudoir, a delicious little retreat hung with Japanese draperies. Reclining gracefully, sometimes hand in hand laid gently,[40] they drink their afternoon stimulants. In delicately cut glasses gin loses much of its vulgarity, but when sportswomen are announced, brandy and sodas are ordered, and telling of adventures and disappointments they watch with dreamy eyes great crabs crawling through the long sea-weeds, and a flight of wild geese that hide with their wings the silver disc of the moon.

As may be supposed, the business could not but suffer by these long hours passed in drunkenness and scandalmongery, but Mrs. Rusville had three daughters to bring out, and she hoped—when she had disposed of her shop, and her feet were set on the redoubtable staircase of Cork Hill[41]—that her aristocratic friend would extend to her a cordial helping hand. Mrs. Rusville is one of the myriad little schemes with which Dublin is honeycombed.

The Castle is the head, the Shelbourne Hotel the body, the Kildare Street Club and Mrs. Rusville's Shop the members of the miserable creature covered with bleeding sores that is called Dublin Society. To-day it trembles with sullen fear, and listens to savage howling of the pack in kennels set in a circle about the Castle, the Hotel, the Club, and the Shop; and as Gladstone advances, the barking springs to meet him; the fierce teeth are heard upon the wood-work. Will he lift the latch and let the hounds rush in on the obscene animal?[42]

AN IRISH COUNTRY HOUSE.

Yes, I am in an Irish country house—in a real Irish country house; there are hundreds like it.[43] A square box-like structure approached by stone steps. On the right and the left are the drawing-room and dining-room. The walls are papered with a hideous French paper, red flowers on a gold ground. The windows are curtained with bright red curtains, scarlet curtains. My host remarks that when they were bought that red was the fashionable colour. There are two flagrantly modern rosewood cabinets nailed against the wall and a few exquisite Chippendale chairs, the value of which no one even remotely suspects. In the dining-room there is a beautiful Chippendale side-board; the walls are hung with pictures of horses whose histories and fortunes are being constantly related to you. Here is the hunter that carried the present squire twenty-five years ago over a six-foot wall; there is the race-horse that ran second for the Chester cup half a century ago; and the present mortgaged condition of the property is owing to the losses sustained on that occasion.

From either side of the house long woods extend like the wings of a theatre, and they embrace a green lawn on which cattle feed. The drive is covered with cow-dung. At the back of the house is a stable-yard with falling roofs and broken doors— an unpaved stable-yard full of pools of water whither pilgrim ducks direct their processions; and further away ensconced in an open place in the laurels is an iron hut in front of which two policemen sit cleaning their rifles. They have been on guard all night and have just been relieved; and their comrades are now walking up and down in front of the house. I can see them as I lean forward to tie my cravat. Mine host has long been under police protection. There is probably no one in Ireland whose life the Land League is so determined to have as his;[44] but being a wise man he never stirs out except when preceded by a car, full of policemen armed to the teeth. These clear the way, and a second car, likewise full of policemen armed to the teeth, follows and guards against his being attacked in the rear. Mine host's unpopularity is easily accounted for. His own property amounts to no more than a thousand a year, and it is mortgaged to the extent of seven hundred a year. The seven hundred must be paid and all reductions must come out of the remaining three hundred. The sins of the fathers descend on the children, and my host's property exists upon paper only. But he has another source of income, he is a land agent and he collects rent to the extent of fifty thousand a year, for which he is paid at the rate of five per cent.[45] To collect so vast a sum from poor people necessitates the serving of writs, evictions, seizures of cattle, etc.; and mine host's pecuniary difficulties force him to do all this remotely. Hence his unpopularity, hence the desire of the National party to remove him. (Remove him is the euphemism in the West for to murder.)

My host's family consists of a wife, three girls, and a son. Two of the girls are tall, strong, ugly young women from three to four and twenty years of age. They think nothing of riding fifteen miles to a hunt, hunting all day and riding home in the evening; and next day they are ready to play a tennis match or to drive thirty miles to a ball. The third girl is a pale little thing with golden hair. She spends her time painting flowers on the panels of the doors and helping her mother with the housekeeping. The son is a type very characteristic of Ireland, and of the present ordering of things in Ireland. We will call him Tom. Tom, after having been in London, where he spent some years in certain vague employments, and having contracted as much debt as his creditors would permit, and more than his father would pay, he had returned home through the Bankruptcy Court and had returned home to wearily drag through life, through days and weeks so appallingly idle that he often feared to get out of bed in the morning. At first his father tried to make use of him in his agency business, and it was principally owing to Mr. Tom's bullying and insolent manners that mine host was now unable to leave his house unless accompanied by police. Tom is about thirty years of age. His legs are long, his hands bony, and stable-yard is written in capital letters on his face. He carries a 'Sportsman'[46] under his arm, a penny and a halfcrown jingle in his pocket; and as he walks he lashes the trousers and boots, whose elegance is an echo of the old Regent Street days, with an ash plant. Given a certain versatility in turning a complimentary phrase, the abundant ease with which he explained, not his ideas, for he had none, but his tastes, which although few were pronounced; add to this the remnant of fashion that still lingers in his wardrobe—scarfs from the Burlington Arcade, scent from Bond Street, cracked patent leather shoes and mended silk stockings—and it will be understood how the girls in this far-away country built something that did duty for an ideal out of this broken-down swell.

After breakfast he begins to chatter. He curses Ireland as the most hideous hole under the sun; he frightens his mother by reiterated assurances that the Land League will leave them as beggars, and, having established this point, he proceeds to develop his plan for buying young horses, training them, and disposing of them in the English market. Eventually he dismisses his audience by taking up the newspaper and falling asleep with the stump of a burnt-up cigarette between his lips. Nothing more is heard of him for an hour; then he is seen slouching through the laurels on his way to the stables; and, whistling to their dogs, his sisters rush after him, their hands thrust into the pockets of their cotton dresses, the mud of the yard oozing through their broken boots. Behind the stables there is a small field lately converted into an exercise-ground, and there the three stand for hours, watching a couple of goat-like colts, mounted by country lads, still in corduroy and hob-nails, walking round and round.

The great argument against the doctrine of eternal punishment is that human nature habituates itself to all things; ample proof of this has been given of late years in the West of Ireland.[47] You would not think it an easy matter to enjoy a shooting party with a policeman walking behind you to prevent a Land Leaguer shooting you while you shot the

pheasant! You would not think it an easy matter to enjoy a
flirtation, with a policeman watching to see that your kissing
was not interrupted by a Land Leaguer sticking a knife into
you from behind—you who spend pleasant lives in the Row,[48]
think that it would be impossible to enjoy love or sport under
such circumstances, but you are wrong! Notwithstanding the
precautions absolutely indispensable if you would preserve a
whole skin, the gentry in Mayo enjoy themselves very well
indeed. And now I hear nothing talked of but a picnic—an
afternoon dance which the people I am staying with are getting
up. It is, I hear, to be given at a house on Lough Carra—'a
house with a splendid floor for dancing,' cries one of the girls.
'And to whom does this house belong?' I ask. 'Oh! to a fellow
who lives in Paris—he never comes here. Pa is his agent, and
we can do what we like with his house.'[49]

As we drove to the picnic we caught glimpses of the lake,
the grey light of the beautiful mere-like lake flashing between
the broken lines of rocky coast and the sloping ridges of the
moorland; and then there are the blue waving lines of the
Clare Mountains[50] drawn in a circle about this landscape, this
barren landscape, so suggestive of savage life and rough and
barbarous minds. For in Ireland you think of border forays,
wild chieftains, and tribes dressed in skins. The graft of civilisation the Anglo-Saxon has for seven hundred years striven to
bind upon the island has never caught, but whether the Celt
will be able to civilise himself when he gets Home Rule I do
not pretend to say. At present he is a savage, eminently fitted
for cattle-lifting, but ill-suited to ply the industry of farming
which the law forces as the alternative of starvation upon him.
Down in the wet below the edge of that bog lies the village.[51]
The cabins are built out of rough stones without mortar. Each
is divided into two, rarely into three, compartments; and the
windows are not so large as those of a railway carriage. And
in these dens a whole family, a family consisting of husband
and wife, grandfather and grandmother, and from eight to ten
children herd together as best they can. The cabins are
thatched or are roofed with green sods cut from the nearest

field. About each doorway there is a dung-heap in which a pig wallows in the wettest and the children play on the driest part. The interior of these cabins can be imagined: a dark place from which exudes a stink; a stink which the inmates describe as a warm smell![52] Around the walls are vague shapes—what, you cannot quite see; like high boxes pushed out of sight are the beds. The floor is broken in places and the rain collects in the hollows, and has to be swept out every morning. A large pig, covered with lice, feeds out of a trough placed in the middle of the floor, and the beast from time to time approaches and sniffs at the child sleeping in a cot by the fireside. The old grandmother waves her palsied hands and the beast retires to his trough.[53] As we have seen the pig, let us see the family at dinner. Of cookery, they have no idea whatever; there is not a single plate or kitchen utensil of any kind in the hovel except the black iron pot that hangs over the fire. The father and mother enter, followed by the brood. The mother, a great strong creature fit for work in the fields, dressed in a red petticoat which scarcely falls below her knees—you see the thick shapeless red legs—lifts the black pot off the fire and carries it to the threshold, one of the children holds a sieve and the water is strained off. Then the pig is hunted under one of the beds, and the family eat their dinner out of the sieve. Cold water from the well washes down this repast; sometimes well-to-do families keep a cow and there is a little butter-milk.[54] These people are called small farmers; they possess from three to ten acres of land, for which they pay from twenty to five-and-twenty shillings an acre. In their tiny fields, not divided by luxuriant hedges like the English fields, but by miserable stone walls which give an unspeakable bleakness to the country, they cultivate oats and potatoes. With the former crop and the pig they pay the landlord, with the latter they live. As Balzac says, 'Les beaux sentiments fleurissent dans l'âme quand la fortune commence de dorer les meubles;'[55] and never have I observed in these people the slightest æsthetic intention—never was a pot of flowers seen in the cottage window of an Irish Celt.[56]

You want to know what Ireland is like? Ireland is like the smell of paraffin oil! The country exhales the damp, flaccid, evil smell of poverty—yes, a poverty that is of the earth earthy. And this smell hangs about every cabin; it rises out of the chimneys with the smoke of the peat, it broods upon the dung-heap and creeps along the deep black bog-holes that line the roadway, and the thin meagre aspect of the marshy fields and the hungry hills reminds you of this smell of poverty—the smell of something sick to death of poverty.

Driving along the bleak roads[57] suddenly we see trees, and through the foliage the grey lake glitters, and its many aspects are unfolded; long wooded promontories, islands, ruined castles, and wide expanses of white water. This is Lake Mount,[58] the property of the mysterious being of whom nothing seems to be known, except that he lives in Paris and writes French poetry. The park is handsome; it is adorned with trees more than a century old, but even here the bitter smell of poverty lingers. The gate-lodge is in ruins, the drive is weed-grown and covered with cow-dung, and herds of cattle wander through the woods and feed along the terraces. The house is very much like the one we have just left: but it is handsomer. Four large pillars support a balcony;[59] the hall door is approached by a wide and imposing flight of steps, and over all there is a huge tablature, on which is written the family motto and the date of the building of the house.[60] Around the gravel-sweep in front of the house, carriages and vehicles of all descriptions are collected, and the protecting policemen and soldiers are talking as naturally of their charges as the nurses do in the Champs-Elysées of their babies! Now a couple leave the group, and, apologising for the intrusion, a policeman reminds a pair of lovers of the danger of pursuing their flirtations into the darkness of the trees.

The day dreams tenderly, and in the genial sunlight the pink dresses of the girls are sweet spots of colour, and the wide lake, with all its reeds and islands and shallowing shores, sparkles like a hand-mirror in the sun.[61] Some of the company stand on the steps feeding their eyes on the summer prospect, others are dancing in the drawing-room to the slangy jingle of a piano;

and the gaiety of the day proceeds without interruption until suddenly appears a singular individual—a young man in a long green coat.[62] His tiny hat, his long hair, his Parisian-cut clothes and his Capoul-like beard give him a very strange and very anomalous air. On the Boulevard he might pass muster, but where he stands he is un *être de féerie*.[63] He is evidently very angry at something; and he rings impatiently. The aged servitor appears.[64]

'What are all these people doing here?'

'This is Mrs. So-and-so's afternoon party, sir. Mr.—— lent the house.[65] I should be very happy to show you over it, but they are dancing in the drawing-room, and lunch is laid out in the dining-room.'

'Show me over the house indeed! Don't you know me; this is my house? I have just returned from Paris.'

'Goodness, gracious, sir!' I beg your pardon; will you go and speak with Mrs.——?

It is easy to imagine the embarrassment of this worthy woman. She could not very well ask the proprietor to give her the pleasure of his company at an afternoon dance in his own house, and on the other hand she could not very well call her guests together, pack up her luncheon, and be off. But the Parisian's heart was one of pity, and seeing how matters stood, he went upstairs, changed his clothes, and begged to be allowed to join in the dance—a permission that was graciously extended to him.

Soon we became friends; soon I was invited to spend a few days with him. He told me his story[66]—that on the refusal of his agent to supply him with any more money he had come over from Paris with a few pounds, and a volume of Baudelaire[67] and Verlaine[68] in his pocket. Of all the latest tricks that had been played with French verse he was thoroughly master; of the size, situation, and condition of his property he knew no more than I did. Indeed, he hated all allusion to be made to it, and he looked forward with positive horror to meeting his tenants, and discussing a reduction of rent with them.[69] This type of man is not unfrequent in Ireland.

THE HOUSE OF AN IRISH POET.

Here we find traces of the riches of other generations—traces that in themselves are characteristic of Ireland. The original design as it shows through the wreck and ruin seems to indicate that from the first all had been undertaken on a scale a little above the fortune of the owner; and this in Ireland! The western Celt is a creature quick to dream, and powerless to execute; in external aspects and in moral history the same tale is told—great things attempted, nothing done; and the physiology and psychology of his country is read in the unfinished pile.[70]

Ireland is a country of abandoned dreams. Here are a few—see this room, it is forty feet square. The floor is of choice French parquet—the walls, stucco of course replaces marble, but in every other respect the room is an exact copy of a Greek chamber.[71] The panels are in mauve and straw colour; and painted in the centre of each panel is a neo-Greek picture. But no curtains fall from the Greek cornices, and the room is furnished with a few bits of heavy and meaningless furniture that would do violence to the taste of a retired soap-boiler.[72] Outside there are terraces and pleasure-grounds laid out according to Italian rule, and the great woods extend from either side down to, and along the shores of, the pale, mild, mere-like lake—a lake that smiles as wearily in the weak sunlight, to use a Balzac simile, *comme une beauté de keepsake dessinée par Westhall,*[73] and this lake is surrounded by amphi-theatrical mountains, and is covered with islands on which you perceive a corner of an old castle, a remnant of the brigandage of old time.[74] But to-day as well as yesterday is in ruins.[75] The great stables once filled with thirty or forty race-horses, are now for the most part but formless masses of brick and mortar: here a bit of roofing still holds on, and there a young ash-tree forces its way through the rack out of which the winner of the Chester cup once drew his hay.[76] And the great wide green path of the race-course that wound in and out through the woods and fields is now overgrown and lost; and the garden where several generations of children played and grew amid everchanging ideas and desires from childhood to manhood, is now but a wild, a sad, and savage place—a strange place where strange weeds overtop the apple closes, and where the roses have returned to the original eglantine. Pushing my way through the jungle I came upon a sun-dial that the sun has not seen these many years, and as I brush away the leaves and earth, and read the markings on the dial, I experience the sensations of awe felt even by him who strives to decipher an inscription upon a lost and forgotten Brahmin tomb. And upon the tall and morose walls, wet with the rain that drips from the overhanging beeches, a peacock—the last of the many generations of peacocks that in gladder days decorated the terraces and the long lawns—now cries dolorously for the pea-hen *morte d'antan*.[77]

And amid these ancient sights my host and I wander: he with his pockets filled with back numbers of 'La Vogue,'[78] from which he occasionally reads sonnets by Mallarmé[79] and Verlaine. And our poetic discussions are prolonged till the hour when in the baronial hall—sad, like the drawing-room, with the sadness of incompleted things—we dine on trout taken that day from the lake, and tiny, half-starved chickens that the *vieux serviteur*[80] procured for us in the village; then in the long evenings we turn over the books in the library—a library to which not a book has been added for the last fifty years: and so the days pass until the hour comes for my friend the Irish poet to go through the dreaded interview with his tenants.

The agent, having lived all his life among bullocks, partook of their animality. His thick legs are encased in gaiters, and he wears a long ulster.[81]

'How do you do?' he exclaimed. 'Do you know that things are getting worse instead of better? There's been another bailiff shot down in Mayo, and we have had a process-sever nearly beaten to death down our side of the country. Gad! I was out with the sub-sheriff and fifty police trying to serve notices on Lord——'s estate, and we had to come back as we went, such blowing of horns you never heard in your life. The whole country was up, and they had a trench cut across the road as wide as a canal.'

'Well, what do you think we had better do with these fellows? Do you think they will take the twenty per cent.?'

''Tis impossible to say. Gad! the League is getting stronger every day. But they ought to take it; twenty per cent. will bring it very nearly down to Griffiths'.' [Griffiths' valuation is a valuation that was made thirty years ago by order of Government for purposes of taxation.]

'But if they don't take it?'

'Well, I don't know what we will do, for notices it is impossible to serve. Gad! I will never forget how we were pelted the other day, such throwing of stones, such blowing of horns! I think you will have to give them the thirty, but we will try them at twenty-five.'[82]

'And if they won't take it?'

'What, the thirty? They will take that, and jumping, you needn't fear. Here they come.'

Turning, the two men watched the forty or fifty peasants, who, with heads set against the wild gusts, advanced steadily up the avenue. The peasants lift their hats, and the interview begins:——[83]

'Now boys,' cries the poet, who thought that a little familiarity would not be inappropriate: 'I have asked you to meet me so that we might come to some agreement about the rents. We have known each other a long time, and my family has been on this estate I don't know how many generations. Therefore—why, of course, I should be very sorry if we had any falling out. I don't know much about farming, but I hear everyone say that this has been a capital year;[84] and now . . . well, I think I cannot do better than to make the same offer as I did before through my agent—that is to say, of twenty per cent. abatement all round—that will bring your rents down to Griffiths' valuation.'

The poet intended to be very impressive; but feeling that words were betraying him he stops short and waits anxiously to hear what answer the peasant who steps forward would make. The old man begins by removing a battered tall hat, out of which falls a red handkerchief; the handkerchief is quickly thrown back into the crown, and at an intimation from the poet hat and handkerchief are replaced on the white head.

'Now, your honour, the rents are too high; we cannot pay the present rent, leastways without a reduction. I have been a tenant on the property, and my fathers before me for the past hundred and fifty years, and it was in '43 that the rents were raised—in the time of your father—the Lord have mercy on his soul!—but he had an agent who was a hard man, and he raised the rents; and since then we have been living on yellow meal[85] and potatoes—potatoes that are watery; there's no diet in them, your honour, and if your honour will come and walk the lands yourself, you will see that I am speaking the truth; we ask nothing better than that you should walk the lands yourself. There are two acres of my land, your honour, flooded for three months of the year, and for that same land I am paying twenty-five shillings an acre. I have my receipts paid down to the last half-year.' And, still speaking, the old man fumbles in his pockets and produces a large pile of papers, which he strives to push into the poet's hand, alluding all the while to the losses he had sustained. Two pigs had died, and he had lost a fine mare and foal.

'I should be delighted to give you thirty per cent. reduction,' cries the poet, as soon as the question of reduction, that had been lost amid schemes for draining and bad seasons, had been re-established. 'But you must remember I have to pay charges, and my creditors won't wait any more than yours will.[86] If you refuse to pay your rents, and I get sold out, you will ruin me, but you won't do yourselves any good; you will have some Englishman here who will make you pay your rents.'

'An Englishman here!' cries a peasant. 'He would go back quicker than he came.'

'Maybe he wouldn't go back at all,' cries another, chuckling. 'We would make an Irishman of him for ever.'

'Begad! we would make him wear the green in real earnest, and a fine sod it would be,' shouted a third.[87]

The witticism is greeted with a roar of laughter, and upon this expression of a somewhat verdant patriotism, the dispute concerning the reduction was resumed.

'Give us the land all round at the Government valuation,'[88] says a man in the middle of the group.

'Why, you are only fifteen per cent. above the valuation,' cries the agent.

For a moment this seems to create a difference of opinion among the peasants; but the League had drawn them too firmly together to be thus easily divided. They talk among themselves in Irish. Then the old man says:

'We can't take less than thirty per cent.; the League would not let us.'

'I can't give you more than twenty.'

'Then let us come home; there is no use our wasting our time here,' cries a sturdy peasant, who, although he spoke but seldom, seemed to exercise an authority over the rest. With one accord they follow him, but rushing forward the agent seizes him by the arm.

'Now then, boys, come back. He will settle with you right enough if you'll only listen to reason.'

Then after a great deal more discussion during which the poet, intensely wearied, strove to recall the tercets of a sonnet by Mallarmé, a bargain was struck, and the tenants agreed to take twenty-five per cent.

But this arrangement by no means ended our poet's troubles. That very evening the agent said, in a pause in the conversation, 'You must see the tenants on all your different properties.'

'On all my different properties? And where are my different properties?'

'You have several properties in the north of Mayo.'[89]

'And where is the north of Mayo?'

'About thirty miles from here. And there you will have an opportunity of visiting the tomb of your ancestor, the man who built this house.'[90]

The poet glanced at the portrait above his head and relapsed into reveries. He seemed however determined to meet his fate.[91] On the following morning a car is waiting for us at the door, and we start on our pilgrimage.[92] During the first eight or nine miles the country presents its usual sad aspect of servitude and poverty. We see on our right and left the same miserable cabins stuck here and there under the potato-fields that feed the family; poor miserable cabins built of loose stones without a tree or a bush to hid their nakedness or shelter the inmates from the wild wet winds—wet with Atlantic surges—that howl up and down the bleak roads and sterile uplands. The children play and pigs wallow on the dung-heap, the woman with her worn red petticoats blowing about her thick red legs, gathers the peat in the brown bog that strikes through the scanty fields, and along the hillsides the woods of the domain lands extend in curving lines, and I see the square white houses of the landlords gleaming at the end of the vistas—handsome square white houses—each is surrounded with a hundred or so of filthy tenements that Providence and God have decreed shall unite and keep the master in affluence and ease. Soon after we enter a small town;[93] the market-place is filled with peasants; a platform has been erected, and, amid a number of green flags, a village orator explains that the landlord whose house he indicates with his finger must not be paid a shilling until he agrees to accept thirty per cent. reduction; the orator is followed by a fat priest who draws subtle distinctions between the different kinds of murder. Two kinds are peculiar to Ireland, he declares: behind-the-wall murder, and eviction murder, and the law of self-preservation is the first law of life.[94] We listen for a few minutes, and then we climb on to the second car that has been prepared for us. The agent sits with a policeman on one side; he thinks if he brought his whole escort it might excite the tenants to refuse to come to terms; the poet and myself sit on the other, the driver sits on a small seat perched over the horse's tail; we are all armed to the teeth. So we enter on a new country, a country bleaker even than the one we left. No landlords live here, they only come here to collect rent. And to find the tenant face to face with nature, removed from the perhaps refining influence of his terrible task-master, is a mournful sight—the mournful grey of these western skies, the morose sterility of these desert hills. We do not readily understand that a cab-horse may find pleasure in life, nor any more do we understand what hopes or aspirations may animate the peasants who live here striving to cultivate this arid land.[95] Now the hills have been left behind and we are passing through an interminable stretch of bog land; and even into this wilderness eviction has forced the peasant. Out in this swamp there are huts, and in the ooze and mud the procreation of the human race is continued. We pass a dwelling-place that strikes me as being the farthest possible limit to which human degradation may be extended. Into the bank formed by the cutting of peat a few poles have been thrust, and on these poles sods of earth have been laid, the front and sides are partly built up with soft black mud. And in this foul den a woman has brought up five children, and in the swamp a few potatoes are cultivated, but the potato crop has failed this year and the family are living on the yellow meal the parish authorities allow them. They are boiling it now in the black iron pot, and will probably eat it out of the pot, for the hut contains nothing but the pot and the straw on which the family sleep. The man in a torn shirt looking like a wild beast is climbing out of the bog hole. 'Whose tenant are you?' I ask. 'M——' he replies, mentioning my host's name,[96] 'but I have received notice to quit.' 'Is not that the best thing that could happen to you?' I ask. 'Why don't you apply to the Tuke fund to be emigrated?'[97]

'My wife likes the old country and we might be worse off in America.'

'But you could not be worse off.'

'Oh, times may mend,' he replies!

How times can mend for him I know not, and I leave him with a picture of most awful poverty burnt for ever in my memory.

Then as we drive to the end of this region of bog, we see a man approaching. It is the bailiff. He tells us that the tenants are waiting to meet us behind that far hill, and there we find ourselves in the presence of thirty or forty men. The agent and the poet get off the car and address them; but it is clear that their minds are made up; they will accept nothing less than thirty per cent. Hoping that the news of their refusal to come to terms will not reach the next property before us we proceed, and some miles farther on a similar scene is re-enacted and with almost similar results.

'It was here your ancestor lived before he went to India and made his fortune,' says the agent. 'The old house is in ruins, and the chapel where he is buried is likewise in ruins; but would you like to see his tomb?'[98]

'Yes, I think I would,' replies the poet; and followed by a group of nearly naked peasants all chattering together, some explaining their differences with their neighbours and begging the landlord to interfere; others insisting on a reduction of rent, because their crops have failed—because 'the potatoes are watery, there is no diet in them'—we approach a ruined chapel. With some hesitation, the reason of which we do not at first understand, one of the peasants shows us the grave-stone almost hidden from sight beneath a monstrous growth of nettles.[99]

After two hundred years the grave has been violated by the peasants for the leaden coffin, and the bones of him who created all that has been wasted—by one generation in terraces,[100] by another in race-horses,[101] and by another in dissipation in Paris,[102] lie scattered about the ground trodden by chance of the passing feet of the peasant.

Notwithstanding his cynicism my friend was touched to the heart. Three days afterwards he began a poem on the subject, the chief merit of which lay in the ingenuity of rhyming Lilith with lit.

THE LANDLORD.[103]

Mr Blake[104] lives in a great square box-like house, placed in the centre of a wet lawn, set about with melancholy trees. The lawn is let to a grazier, and herds of cattle feed even to the hall door. The beasts tramp through the laurels, across the terraces, and the walks are covered with cow-dung; every ornamental fence has been broken down, the cut stone has slipped out of the corner walls of the stable and garden, and in slush, neglect, and ruin the aspect of these places is that of a decaying farmyard. If you pull the shaky bell-handle you will hear a mournful ringing far away down in the distant corridor; you will be kept waiting a long time, but eventually the butler, an old, shabby, and decrepit creature, whose life has been passed in ever-humbling servitude, will open the door to you. He is now dressed in his master's old clothes—they are three sizes too large for him, and the sleeves of the coat are turned up some five or six inches. Like everything else in Ireland he bears signs of better days; and, through all the shabbiness and all the poverty, you see the fashionable London servant. He is the rat that has not left the sinking ship, and he has starved even to this. Still there is an air of fashion in the way he shows you into the drawing-room—a fadingly furnished room—heavy antique chairs and sofas, a broken piano, and some lamentable pictures of dogs going after birds. This was good enough for yesterday, it is good enough for to-day, and to-morrow we may not be here. You sit on a sofa which seems to be stuffed with the national potato, and you seek for something to read. There is nothing but the 'Freeman's Journal,'[105] and mechanically you glance through the daily list of outrages until a worn and uninteresting lady enters. Platitude is read in every gesture, trouble in every look; she introduces you to her six children, and asks you to have a cup of tea. An effort is made to speak of London, but in a few minutes the conversation has lapsed into the usual and never-ceasing wailing concerning the prospects of the country—in other words the chances of collecting rent.

The story of Mr. Blake's life is as follows:—When he came of age his father made him an allowance of three hundred a year, and sent him to London to see the world and if possible to pick up an heiress. He took a couple of furnished rooms in Duke Street, St. James's, and then came the whelming desire to eat of the fruit and gather the flowers of life—to dine in fashionable places, to feel delicately dressed, to be *chic*, to avoid the public road of dust and heat, and choose a pleasant by-path adorned with flowers and where but few are seen . . . All Irish gentlemen are sportsmen. Mr. Blake has a friend in a hunting county, and to bring a couple of horses and go and stay with him is the first step. Mr. Blake is a first-rate rider, the horses turn out well, and he sells them for twice as much as he gave for them. He buys some more and disposes of them on equally advantageous terms. He repeats the trick again and again, with varying success, until at the end of the season he returns to London crazed with the money he has made, with pleasure, with flattery, and a prospect of gay life.[106] Having some hundreds of pounds in the bank he henceforth pays a pound a day for a handsome[107] apartment and he goes to the Gaiety Theatre. . . .

At the Gaiety Theatre he meets Maud. Maud, who sings in the chorus or dances in the ballet, delights in supper parties, and is insatiable as regards the number of her admirers.[108] For some months he enjoys the privilege of paying Maud's bills and being constantly at her side. About August Mr. Blake begins to look anxiously to the hunting season as a means of replenishing his exhausted exchequer. This time he goes down to Northamptonshire with five horses, but the horses fall lame, he loses his money at cards, everything goes wrong, and there is nothing to do but to have recourse to the Jews. Luck comes again and luck goes again, but the expenses remain the same,[109] and at last the end comes, and there is the usual storm of sighs and bitter recriminations. Nevertheless at his club that evening Mr. Blake comes to the conclusion that after all it was perhaps for the best, indeed a glance at his bank-book convinces him that the rupture came not one hour too soon—and marriage loomed above the horizon. Henceforth Mr. Blake is a reformed man. He calls on the Jesuits in Farm Street, and he is seen at various luncheon parties in Bayswater; and for a year he made love to every girl he met in the hopes she might be the heiress whose fortune would pay off the mortgages that 'to a certain extent crippled the property.' But the heiress never came, and if she did she was invariably engaged to some one else; and the money-lenders were pressing, so pressing that after five years' dissipation Mr. Blake had to return home to economise; and soon after his broken-hearted father—who had lived in London and returned home some thirty years ago in exactly the same way—died, leaving his son to get out of the money-lenders' clutches as best he could. But six thousand pounds is a large sum, and press the tenants as he would, though he might demand premiums for the letting of every farm, Mr. Blake found that if he wanted to make both ends meet he would have to deprive himself of every pleasure—that is to say he would have to live in Roscommon all the year round; at the most he could not hope to spend more than a fortnight in London. He can still keep a couple of horses, he can get as much shooting and tennis-playing as he desires, and for six months his longing for London is neither bitter nor profound. There is only one thing that troubles him, and that is a haunting and irritating remembrance of Maud, not perhaps of the Maud he knew and admired in the Strand,[110] for his love once so personal has now become catholic. . . .[111]

A young unmarried landlord is an object of the keenest interest to the peasant women of Ireland; so soon as he settles down to live at home, the drama commences. The mother and the comely daughter are loitering at the hall-door. The door opens, and the young master appears. He admires the girl's rosy cheeks and takes an interest in her.[112] Three days after when he is out shooting he meets the girl. She tells him she wants to go out to service, speaks of going to England. He easily dissuades her, and takes her in as housekeeper.[113] Biddy's brothers are transferred from the fields to the stables, and some become grooms, bailiffs, and gamekeepers.

Five years bring five children. Mr. Blake is weary of his numerous dependents, and he is harassed by debts. The money-lender has been paid, but other debts have been contracted and are pressing on him sorely. How is he to relieve himself? There is no way but marriage. A neighbour has an elderly daughter whom he has never been able to get rid of; he is a rich grazier and he can give her seven thousand pounds down. Seven thousand pounds is Eldorado to embarrassed Mr. Blake, and he proceeds at once to come to terms with Biddy and Biddy's family. The father-in-law declares that he could not hear of their remaining in the country, to America they must go if the marriage is to be, and to America Biddy and her five children are sent, the brothers elect to start for England, the father and mother are given twenty pounds, and Mrs. Blake takes the place vacated by the discarded Biddy.[114]

About every landlord's house in Ireland traces are found of immorality with peasant women, and it is curious to note the proportion of tenants that bear the landlords' names, and often at a petty sessions the magistrate will not convict the prisoner because he knows Blake to be his half-brother or his son.

.   .   .   .   .

Sometimes, before the birth of her eleventh child, the landlord takes Biddy to church, and puts the ring on her finger, and the baby who is born two months after is legitimate and heir to the property—and title, if there be one in the family. The young landlord grows up amid his illegitimate brothers and sisters, for whom the father is striving to lay by a few thousand pounds. I know of no novelist who has touched this subject, and yet how full it is of poor human nature: vice, degradation, pity, hard-heartedness, grow on its every branch like blackberries in an autumn hedge.

.   .   .   .   .

The first three or four years that succeeded his marriage were happy ones; Ireland was quiet, rents were paid, and his wife's fortune had relieved Mr. Blake of his personal debts. But in '77 came the periodic failure of the potato crop,[115] and the people starved. Enactments were issued by the thousand, and the country was about to be depopulated again as it was before in '49.[116] He who knows Ireland knows what it is to pass from a region where the hovels are plentiful, and the gaunt hill-sides are divided into patches by walls—loose round stones piled one on top of the other—to a region of wide pasture lands where herds upon herds of bullocks graze. Look at the fragment of ruined cottage, and think of the misery and woe. Family after family were dug out with crowbar and pick, as if they were rabbits, and were driven forth to die or to find their way to America. Many died, but the survivors and their sons are now wealthy men in New York, Chicago and Boston; and it is they who supply Parnell with money to prosecute to exile and ruin the war against landlordism.

I am a landlord to-day, but I will recognise it as a fact that had not Davitt organised the Land League in '78, a great clearance of peasants would have been again made in '78.[117] Mr. Blake is not a hard-hearted man, but in Ireland we are accustomed to evictions, and no doubt he would have cleared his property of as many tenants as possible, and have re-organised it on a system of grazing. For since '49 every good landlord regrets his goodness; when we pass the great tracts of pasture land with the fragment of ruined cottage we say in our hearts: 'Oh that I had, or my father had, evicted like the others in '49!'[118]

Mr. Blake's estate is one of the worst in the West of Ireland; Mr. Blake has two hundred tenants, there is not a man on the estate who is worth a hundred pounds, and most of his tenants live out on the verge of the bog, where they till a few wretched acres of land, and for which they pay on an average from four to five pounds a year. Mr. Blake's rental stands at two thousand a year, but his father who kept race-horses put a mortgage of five per cent. on the estate, for which five per cent. interest is paid a year. Then the widow is in receipt of three, and the younger children of two, hundred a year;[119] Mr. Blake's agent takes five per cent. of the gross rental, for Mr. Blake must have an agent, it is the custom in Ireland to have agents, and this is so partly because the landlords are too fine gentlemen to do their own business, partly because a third person can deal more summarily with the tenants than the landlord. In '81 the Land Act knocked three hundred more off his income,[120] leaving, when taxes and bad debts are deducted, something about four hundred a year for our typical landlord to live on. For, mark you, all losses must be borne by the unfortunate Mr. Blake—all bad debts, and the forcible reduction of rent ordained by the Land Act of '81 come out of his pocket—the mortgagees, the widow and the younger children lose not one penny, no matter what disastrous seasons time may bring; no matter what Radical Land Bills Mr. Gladstone or Mr. Parnell may force through the House of Commons; and yet they, mortgagees, widow, and younger children all draw their income from the same source as the landlord. Herein lies, it seems to me, the great injustice of the Land Bill of '81 and likewise of the Bill on which Mr. Parnell is speaking [121] as I write this very line; if rents are reduced by State intervention, no distinction should be made in proprietorship—mortgagees, widow, etc., should bear a proportional loss.

But will the margin that the Land Act of '81 left to the proprietor, will it continue to be paid? This is the terrible 'To be or not to be' that now gnaws at every landlord's heart, and most of all at Mr. Blake's; for he has six children to support, and he is now forty and incapable of earning a shilling unless perhaps as a common labourer. Is it possible that the entire upper class of a country will be deprived of all its worldly goods and turned adrift out on the world to starve, and that we shall soon have a country composed exclusively of peasants? Never has the world seen, no not even France in time of revolution, such a reversal of fortune as that which is threatened in Ireland. And it is far from certain that this change in the affairs of men will not come to pass. Ireland is now quiet;[122] at the sign of Mr. Parnell murder and violence have ceased, but when he finds that he and his party are powerless to obtain Home Rule he will say, like Pilate, 'I will wash my hands of the blood of these men;' and then outrage and murder will again make the land horrible, and the tenant-farmers will dictate their terms to the landlords and those of his already enfeebled class, whom the assassin scare will gradually starve to death or exile.

THE TENANT-FARMER.

Micky Moran is a tenant-farmer. His holding consists of ten acres of land, not set in one compact flat about the cabin which he built himself by the roadside, but scattered here and there through the surrounding farms: to get at his oat-field he has to cross his neighbour's potato-garden, and this right of way is conducive, as may be easily imagined, to fierce disputes.[123]

The sun is setting behind the blue band of mountains, the islands with their hanging shadows shove their black noses like fish through the motionless silver of the lake, and now the pale elusive distance floats away in long curving lines, in tones of grey and rose; the quacking of the ducks in the reeds adds an exquisite stillness to the scene. But suddenly the sonorous shores resound with oaths, and the tranquil evening is rent with screams for vengeance; women rush for pitchforks and spades, the children crowd out of the filthy hovel, and Micky Moran has much difficulty in escaping with his life.

Micky Moran is a strong-built man of forty-five: a pair of corduroy trousers, a frieze coat, a dark discoloured skin with scanty whiskers, a snub nose, blue eyes set deep under a low forehead, receding temples and square-set jaws. His face is expressive of meanness, sullenness, stupidity; he is obviously nearer to the earth than the Saxon; he reminds me of some low earth-animal whose nature has not yet risen from out the soil.[124] He is evidently of a degenerate race—a race that has been left behind—and should perish, like the black rat perished before the brown and more ferocious species.[125] Micky is not a Celt, he is a Fin. Ages ago the Fins were defeated by the Celts and driven into the outlying districts of Connaught; there they should have died, but owing to their extraordinary power of reproduction they are now making headway against the superior races.[126] If pestilence or war do not intervene, families of ten will win the battle of existence for the most ill-favoured race that ever trod the earth. And Micky's and his wife's philoprogenitiveness is quite up to the average; they are ten in the family. His eldest son and daughter are in America, the two next are working in different employments in Manchester, at home there is a baby in arms, three children, three, four, and six years of age, a boy of seventeen and Mary a girl of eighteen. Poor Mary! She went in for making a big catch and got herself into trouble.

The Irish peasants are the most moral people in the world. Their morality fails only when their landlord covets their daughter, and that custom being a survival of the serfdom of the past is rapidly dying out. But in certain parishes where the ruling of the priest is feeble, the young girls in order to get husbands allow themselves to be seduced, counting on the influence that will be brought to bear on the young man that he will marry them afterwards. In all other ways they are as I say the most moral (using the word moral in its limited, not its general, sense) people in the world. And this special morality is necessitated by their mode of living, their ignorance, their superstition. For to save their flocks from sin—I mean the sin the most generally hateful to the spirit and teaching of the Catholic Church—the priests encourage early marriages; in Ireland you seldom see a young man who is not married,[127] and there is in all classes a very general absence of any practical theory of life, and much dull acquiescence in the belief that God does not bring life into the world without providing for it.[128] If you bear this in mind, and if you take into account that the Irish peasant has lived for centuries in a damp, black, miserable hole from which he was expelled if he did not give up his daughter, if he did not vote as the agent told him, you will begin to understand why he is grossly superstitious and stupidly improvident, and why he breeds blindly like a newt in the wet and the slime. The Irish race is one that has been forgotten and left behind in a bog hole; it smells of the wet earth, its face seems as if made of it, and its ideas are moist and dull, and as sterile as peat.

A dim idea floats in the minds of the young men that they had better leave home, that there is not much to do, not much to hope for in the plot of ground that they till on a hillside of this far western land; but the agitator comes along and declares that Ireland is for the Irish, that her children must not go away. The young man thinks over what he has heard at the meeting, and as he walks home he stops to speak to his neighbour's daughter. He admires her rosy cheeks, and her hideous thick red legs do not strike him as abominable, for he has never seen others; he meets her the following evening and they pass from the lane into the shadows of the fields.[129] Why detail the sequel? Mary knows that in due time her father, mother, and above all the priest, will intervene, and that the young man will be forced to marry her. In ninety-nine cases out of a hundred these tactics prove successful, but Mary is the exception that proves the rule.[130] Actuated by the laudable desire to do as well for herself as possible, she made eyes at the best *parti* in her village—a young man whose father farmed something like thirty acres of land. Up to a certain point everything went as well and as successfully with Mary as the most hopeful Irish maiden could desire.[131] As to the present there had been nothing extravagant or eccentric in Mary's conduct; she had proceeded on the most approved principles, and her father and mother looked upon her with love and respect, seeing in her the wife of their rich neighbour, and they waited anxiously for the time to come when she would throw herself into their arms and confess her sad condition. When this occurred about three months after,[132] like good parents that they were, they took immediate steps to rehabilitate their daughter in the opinion of the world. They went round to see the father of the young man, who declared his son to be as innocent as the new-born babe, or rather as the babe un-born. The priest was applied to; but he was of the old school, a quiet man who loved his Latin authors and his glass of punch, and his denunciation of the young man from the altar did not seem to change anything in the young man's determination, and the publication of the banns seemed as far off as ever. Threats and violence were then resorted to, the outraged parents summoned their cousins and their uncles, and a moonlight expedition was spoken of; but the young man was a prominent member of the League, and the project had to be abandoned. The young man continued to deny the seduction, and when at last it became clear that he could not be forced into marrying, the fallen woman was driven from the hearth she had disgraced, and told to make her way to the workhouse, the proper place for her to bring her bastard brat into the world.[133]

I shall not forget the last time I saw Mary. She was living on the confines of the village in a hollow in the hill-side built about with rough stones and covered with clods of earth; a still more horrible dwelling-place than the one she had been driven from, with an old woman who had been a priest's servant. There she had been delivered of her child. No one speaks to her; and in the morning and evening you see her sitting under the hawthorn tree, sole tree of that wild landscape.[134] She nurses the child, and her thighs and bosom are bare, and the wind is full of her wailing, and as you turn and see her sitting—lonely, oh! so lonely—she is as touching a picture of human misery as the mind of man can conceive.[135]

.   .   .   .   .

I have said that Micky Moran's farm consists of ten acres of land.

For these ten acres he used to pay a yearly rent of nine pounds five shillings, but the Land Act of '81 reduced his rent to seven pounds. An acre and a half is devoted to potatoes, three acres and a half to oats, and the remainder is in grass on which he feeds a few sheep and a yearling calf. The sheep generally die, and the calf often dies, and if the milk does not fail the family lives upon yellow meal which is bought with the money the daughter sends home from America, where she works as a kitchen-maid, and the money the son sends from Manchester, where he works as a barman in a public-house. And here I must say a word in praise of the conduct of the Irish children towards their parents. Never do they forget them;

I have known sons and daughters who have been away in America for ten, yes and fifteen, years, and who regularly send home their savings to the old couple in Ireland. But how does Micky Moran pay his rent? Some of the rent comes from America and Manchester, some from the sale of the pig, and then Micky Moran goes to England every year to do harvest work, and if he is lucky he returns with half-a-dozen pounds.[136] The farm, although it be not a profitable concern, is at least a plot of ground where the wife may bear children and the pig may wallow. From our point of view Micky Moran's life has been neither pleasant nor successful. He was born in the darkness and damp of a hovel, and excepting the months of the year when he goes to England to earn the rent, he has lived in it. Moreover he and his father before him have lived in daily and nightly fear of being evicted from their horrid home; for the possibility of the Moran family being able to supply the yearly demands of the agent has never been even at best of times more than a bare possibility. Since his name was substituted for his father's in the agent's book, he has received innumerable notices to quit, and his sheep and his pig and his calf have been seized for rent on many occasions. But by making great sacrifices he has always been able to keep a roof over his head.

It was however a very bad year for poor Moran; everything went against him: the potato crop had failed, his pig and his sheep had died. Then he wrote to his sons in Manchester, and to his daughter in New York, but the young people could not make up the money, and the sheriff's officers were at the broker's door. Micky Moran threw himself into the arms of the League that were extended to save him. Moran was saved. The agent was fired at, and when the sheriff's officers, protected by a hundred police, came to evict, they were met by some thousand people who pelted them with stones and forced them to retreat. Henceforth Micky Moran understood his power; in company with the other tenants he attended the agent and told him flatly that they would pay no rent unless they were allowed a reduction of twenty-five per cent. 'We do not expect the land for nothing,' they said, 'but we must have it at a fair rent'.

So it was that Micky Moran first defied the law; but his connection with crime did not end here. The son who remained at home now goes out every night for a walk on the road; and not to meet a girl, but half-a-dozen young fellows like himself, varying in age from eighteen to twenty-six. Sometimes they go to the public-house which Balzac in his novel 'Les Paysans'—that most wonderful anticipation of the phenomena of the Irish crises—calls 'the people's parliament,'[137] but more often they go to each other's houses, where they sit and talk till midnight. Now they are at Moran's. A great peat fire is blazing on the hearth, and the licking red flames and the heaps of white ash are a picturesque decoration; and then the sheep-dog curled up in beautiful attitude, the sharp nose resting on the paws, his long coat glistening. The chins and hands of the speakers stand out in trenchant contrast, and the squalor of the background is concealed in romantic shadow. The mother and younger children have gone through the hole of the dividing wall, and the bed in which the girl sleeps is vague and shadowy. The men speak in Irish and in undertones; they sit round the fire on logs of wood, and they are drawn close together. Mickey smokes in the chimney corner, and sullenly acquiesces in what is said. The young men are bolder than he, and he fears that there will be, as he puts it, 'Bad work done before long.' In truth the conversation does seem a little dangerous. They are talking of their landlord's bailiff.

'If it weren't for that son of a ——,[138] Ferick, Mr. Blake would give us the thirty per cent.'

'He would; but Ferick can do what he likes with him: hasn't he got the best land in the parish?'

'Wasn't it only ten years ago that he took up five acres from which Widow Flanagan was evicted?'[139]

'And he would do the same again if he had the chance.'

'He thinks he'll be a landlord one of these days in the parish. Don't they say he has five hundred pounds put away in the bank?'

'And haven't you heard that he has an ejectment decree out against Patrick Murphy, your uncle? and if he gets him put out he will take up the land.'

'He nor the likes of him will never take up Patrick Murphy's land, not as long as there's lead to be bought in Ireland.'

'He would walk on us all if he could, but I think his time is nearly up.'

'It is as if he has taken out a decree against Patrick Murphy, and no mistake.'

'I will for one, and I think there are a couple of boys in the parish.'

'Begorra, he must be got rid of! We can stand him no more.'

'We might get some help from the League; leastways we might ask what the League thinks of him. We will speak to Daly after mass next Sunday. I don't think he knows that there is a decree out against Patrick Murphy.'

This conversation caused Micky Moran much anxiety, and had he been able he would have prevented his son from attending Mass on the following Sunday. But the boy was obstinate, and then Micky reflected that to lose Mass——

Inherited beliefs and customs, profitable although their rejection may be, cannot be put aside at will by force of will, and some years will elapse before Micky and his likes will say that the land they till is theirs, and will by force of numbers— by that force that having nothing to lose brings—will gradually terrify the mortgaged landowners into bankruptcy; but sooner or later this will come to pass, and then, when the estates are put up for auction, Micky Moran and his like will terrify, with assassination and threats of assassination all intending purchasers away—will, in fine, by an intermittingness of effort, win back to the Celt the land that was taken from the Celt.

THE PRIEST.

Father Tom Shannon is the son of a village grocer. Having shown more than ordinary intelligence at school it was hoped that he would devote himself to patriotism, but being of a sober, mild, and retiring disposition, it was eventually decided that he was more fitted to being a priest. Priesthood and patriotism are the only ways of advancement open in Ireland to those who are not landlords. Father Tom was therefore sent to Maynooth. (Maynooth is a college subventioned by the State for the education of those who intend to enter the Irish priesthood.) There he remained six years learning Latin and theology. He was ordained when he was twenty-three, and immediately after he was allotted a curacy among the mountains, and when he had served God for about ten years in this humble position the bishop gave him a parish, and this is the highest position he may hope to attain to.

Let us look at his house. It is a long cottage, whitewashed and solidly thatched, and stands in a green field: it faces the high road. The door is painted, the windows are three feet by four, and a spray of woodbine clambers about one corner; there are a few trees and a paling. It is clean—it is, in a word, inhabitable; it is the one point in the vast abyss which lies between the hovels of the peasants and the large square houses of the landlords. There is a little brass knocker on the door; you knock, and the priest's servant—they are all the same, nondescript women of fifty—dressed in a red petticoat—barely covering her naked legs, her shoulders are covered with a shawl, opens the door, and saluting you with a curtsey, asks you to walk into the parlour. You are in the very narrowest of passages, and you are conscious that there are all sorts of rooms about you—rooms run up hurriedly with ill-fitting boards and rudely papered. These arrangements were necessary, for Father Shannon has three sisters dependent upon him for support, and the promiscuity of the cabin is not possible in the priest's house. The shutting of doors and the flying steps you heard as you waited on the doorstep were the three sisters leaving the parlour. For more than all else the Irish priest is diffident of his female relations, and he anxiously keeps them out of sight as much as possible. The lot of these poor women is a hard one: they cannot associate with the peasant women, and if the Catholic landlord would strain a point and invite them to an occasional lunch party, their brother would not allow them to accept. And the same scrupulousness pervades his entire conduct in his relations with women. Shakespeare says: 'For one chaste man I will show you twenty lascivious turtles,'[140] but this was because Shakespeare did not know the Irish priesthood. They may, and they no doubt do, occasionally get drunk, and it cannot be denied that their utterances on the altar savour strongly of incentive to murder, but of other immorality[141] they know nothing. Their behaviour on this point is most curious indeed, and how so large a body of men can live so free from reproach would prove an interesting subject for physiological and psychological analysis. That they sin and elude discovery, no one who knows the country, no one who knows how they live apart, every eye fixed upon them, would believe for a moment.[142] It is said that they undergo a fortifying discipline for two years at Maynooth, which exceeds in severity that endured by the early Fathers of the Church.[143]

In Father Tom's parlour there is a fragment of ragged carpet, a small bookcase, some dilapidated chairs, and a piano. Father Tom is a large, heavy man, he walks with stomach advanced—there is much ostentation in his walk, there is treachery in the long warm squeeze of his hand, and dissimulation in the unctuous words of welcome with which he greets you. But Father Tom is better than the first impression would lead you to believe; he is no doubt arrogant, vain, and his intelligence, notwithstanding the parade he makes of it, you soon perceive is limited and of a common kind. He affects an interest in literature, he alludes to pictures he has read or is acquainted with through the medium of engravings, but it is

not until the conversation becomes political that Father Tom
comes forth fully fledged in all the glory of patriotism and
priesthood. He speaks of all the principal Members of the
House of Commons by name, and on the slightest provocation
he will explain to you their views and the arguments with
which they uphold their views.[144] He astonishes you with his
knowledge of Free Trade, and he bewilders you with the
reasons that may be adduced for the adoption of some sort of
protection tariff; and his lengthened discourse is broken up by
'Now do take a glass of wine . . . let me run and get you a
glass of wine . . . now you must take a glass of wine . . . do
you prefer port or sherry? After your walk I am sure you
would like a glass of wine' . . . and even when you have taken
up your hat and stick he will hold your hand in his large fat
paw, and continue to press you to drink, and as you walk
away you hear him crying after you . . . 'I wish you would,
you must not go away without having had a glass of wine.'

You have talked a great deal with Father Tom, and you
saw that he was nervously anxious to prove to you that he was
in no way behind time, that he was in every sense of the word
up to date. Father Tom was very anxious to convince you of
his modernity, and curiously enough this is the very quality
that he is lacking in. Ireland has moved rapidly in the last
eight or nine years, many have been left behind in the race,
and Father Tom, although he is far from suspecting it, is one
of these. Father Tom is a compromise between the priest of
the last generation—the benign old man who loved his Horace
and prepared his favourite landlord's sons for a public school
in England,[145] and the drunken demagogue of the present day
who preaches assassination[146] from the altar. The majority of the
priests of Ireland are of Father Tom's persuasion. He believes
in nearly all that is supposed to represent progress: peasant
proprietors, fair rents, and Home Rule; he will denounce
land-grabbing—(land-grabbing is willingness to take land
from which another has been evicted)—but Father Tom is a
little diffident about accepting the principle of boycotting.
And here I must beg leave to make a digression and explain

the meaning and the origin of the word boycotting. Captain Boycott is a friend and neighbour of mine in the West. He is as fine a sportsman as I ever knew, a fearless rider and an excellent shot; a man who never bestowed a passing thought on immortality of any kind, and when it was violently thrust upon him, strove to the best of his power to shirk the responsibility. It was in the autumn of 1879, that Captain Boycott, who was then Lord Erne's agent, declared, in spite of all warning, that he would collect his lordship's rents if there was law in the land. When his determination to evict at all cost and all risk became known it was reported through the county that the Captain had been to London, and had strongly advised Lord Erne against giving any reduction whatever. This was not to be borne, and when the news reached the head office of the League, in Dublin, advice was sent to Mayo that pressure should be put on the people, that Captain Boycott's servants should be forced to leave him, that no one should sell him bread, food, or wine; that his crops should be left to rot in the fields. These counsels were received with enthusiasm, and acted upon vigorously. Soon it required a hundred police to save the Captain from assassination, and when labourers came from the North to save his crops the anger of the peasants waxed louder, and their resolution not to miss their vengeance became more and more marked. I shall never forget when I saw a regiment of soldiers encamped on the poor man's lawn, and he, looking like a hunted animal walking up and down between the huts, a repeating rifle under his arm, two revolvers and a long dagger in his belt.[147] Like a comet the verb 'to boycott' appeared, it was passed from mouth to mouth, it was caught up by the reporter, and passed on to the leader writer;[148] soon after it appeared in magazines and books, and within two years of its birth it was as firmly established as any word in our language, and every future lexicographer will have to include it. To-day it is not considered slang, and would be used by our most elegant writers. The ready adoption of this word seems to indicate the rapid advance of the Irish struggle and the inevitableness of Irish idea in the future.

It is Sunday morning. High up in the cold air the chapel-bell is clanging harshly, and the reverberation travelling over stony upland and boggy plain summons the villagers to Mass.[149] They are coming along the grey roads, and they stand against those endless grey stone walls to let the landlord's carriage pass. The women and girls carry their boots and stockings in their hands; from long custom they prefer to walk bare-footed. Presently they will find a bare corner where they will finish their toilet. The very old men are dressed in the traditional tailcoats and breeches; they pass, mumbling their toothless gums, evidently a little troubled by the new ideas and the new action of Ireland of to-day.[150] The chapel gate is plastered with bills announcing a Land League meeting; and, standing on the grave-stones, the young men watch the great lumbering carriage of a neighbouring landlord drive up to the door. They guess how annoyed he will be at the sight of the proclamations calling on the tenant-farmers to assemble in thousands and put down the land-grabbers, and the land-thieves. And they are right; the landlord looks abashed, he seems ashamed of his fine carriage, and he is terrified like someone who knows his doom is written, although it has not been spoken judicially.

The young men we saw talking round Micky Moran's fire are now grouped round a tombstone, and in veiled words and covert insinuation they discuss the necessity for Ferick's 'removal'. Apparently they are asking the advice of Daly, a tall young man who stands by, one foot on the tomb, listening attentively. In dress and manner he seems a little superior to the others. He is careful not to answer any of the questions that are put to him, and he advances no opinion except that if all they say is true, and he has heard as much in another quarter, 'that Ferick ought to be boycotted.' He leans to the opinion that boycotting is better than 'removal'. As he speaks he turns to cast a contemptuous look at the priest who is passing towards the door of the sacristy.

Father Tom is proud, ostentatious, overbearing, and it is maddening to him to know that there exists anyone in the

parish who dares to sneer at his authority. It has been
whispered that young Daly does not believe in God, and
thinks priests should be prosecuted under the Vagrancy Acts.
What evil so poisonous as this? The flame of Father Tom's
hatred is blown red; he will crush this viper, he will stamp out
this impudent upstart; there shall be no followers of Voltaire in
his parish; to pervert the minds of the young from the truths
of the Holy Roman Catholic Church.[151] What was this upstart
talking of? No doubt preaching infidelity or plotting outrage
on man or beast. Ferick has been threatened and it is well
known that his life is in danger; murder is forgiven in the
confessional, but for wilful infidelity there can be no salvation.
Then the agitation against rent is exceeding its natural limits, for
now the tenant-farmers refuse to pay the village shop-keepers
as readily as they do the landlords—Father Tom's parents are
grocers.[152] Alarmed at the steady increase of outrages in his
parish, and indignant at the opposition that was offered to the
shop-keepers when they attempted to enforce their claims by
law, Father Tom for some time back had been considering the
Land Question from a different side.

.   .   .   .   .

He who has not attended Mass in an Irish Chapel cannot
judge of Irish life;—its three or four aspects are strangely
reflected and sharply epitomised in that fugitive hour. You
have the Irish landscape well in your mind's eye—the grey sky
and blue mountains in a ring, the hovels, the grey stony
uplands, and the miles of brown bog where the curlews are
flying. Say then, if it is not parcel of this gaunt white chapel,
through whose broken windows the swallows fly circling? In
the middle of the earthen floor there is a rude font for holy
water, and in their haste and devotion the peasants splash the
water so that it seems like an *abreuvoir*[153] where cattle have
been lately drinking. There are a few pews; those next to the
Communion rails are reserved for the landlords. The fluff on
the bended neck of the girl is gold in the beam of white light

that falls across the chapel, she prays gracefully, with refinement, addressing God in sweet and conventional phrases,
and the delicate odour of *verveine*[154] rises out of silk and fur and
evaporates; the peasant women wrapped in their long black
cloaks are bent double over the pews; their thin, long, yellow
hands extended beyond their faces clutch a rosary feverishly;
some of the men are down on their hands and knees
grovelling, some kneel with straight backs, chins lifted, breasts
advanced—poses that recall those of martyred saints; they
groan, they strike their breasts, their hearts are full of the gross
superstition of the moment, they address God in the coarse
language of the cabin; out of their torn shirts, revealing the
beast-like hair of their breasts, rises the rancid sweat of the
fields; and the sour smells of frieze and the heavy, earthy smells
of the cabin are as an almost palpable dust in the intense
morning light as it flows through the windows. They cough
and groan as they pray, and the spittle splashes on the floor.

Father Tom continues his murmuring[155] at the altar, and as
he mumbles through the well-known Latin, he chews the cud
of his vengeance: once for all he will stamp out the evil thing
that has grown up in his parish. And as he turns round to
preach as is customary before the last gospel, the peasants, like
a herd advancing, tramp up the church to get well within
hearing. He begins by deploring the outrages that have lately
taken place in his parish, he dwells on the terrible punishment
that awaits those who commit murder, and then, resolved to
strike a severe blow, he says, taking a piece of money from his
pocket, 'Give unto Cæsar what belongs to Cæsar and to God
what belongs to God.'[156] But the people do not understand,
and when, to explain himself, Father Tom tells them that they
should pay their lawful debts, they walk, Mr. Daly at their
head, out of the chapel. Father Tom's pride suffered terribly;
it was a sore blow to be thus rebuked in his own chapel, and
it was a worse one to be told that his congregation did not
care to hear politics preached from the altar. And a few days
after he was asked to take the chair at a Land League meeting;
he refused, urging that he could not stand on the platform

with men who were in the habit of impressing on the tenant-farmers that they should pay their landlords with lead and not with gold; whereupon he was politely informed that if he did not attend the meeting he would be paid no dues that year.

Father Tom knows that the Land League is Socialism, and that Socialism is atheism, but the need of the moment is the greatest need of all, and he goes to the meeting striving to arrange a middle course, striving to adapt murder to his cloth. He declares that murder is unnecessary, and then he says that it is against the law of God, and then he argues that there are two kinds of murder: the murder committed by the landlord when he turns a whole family to die in the ditch in the middle of winter, and the murder committed by the father of the family when he hides behind a wall and shoots the landlord as he drives past in his carriage. Father Tom does not like land meetings, his heart and conscience revolt against them; the landlords pay him well, it would be a great loss to him to lose them, and he would miss his Sunday dinner in the 'big house;' so considering all these things Father Tom strives, as we say here, to sit on the two stools—as they say in France *de ménager la chèvre et les choux*.[157]

THE PATRIOT.

James, when he was ten years old was running bare-footed to the National School, and as he ran he touched his little cap to every landlord who passed him on the road. But he was a sharp lad, and he soon attracted the priest's attention. The priest was one of the last generation—a kind old man who loved his Horace and did not interfere, save when begged to intercede with the landlord in favour of a penniless tenant, or when he threatens to denounce a young man from the altar if he does not marry the girl he has seduced. It amuses him to teach his beloved Latin; he has prepared two or three of his favourite landlord's sons for the public schools in England, but they are away now, and he sees no outlet for his charity but little James. The boy is called in, and henceforth he spends his mornings with the priest. And although he does not make much progress in Latin—(he is of that temper which disdains all which it does not see can be turned to practical and immediate account)—he profits largely by his relations with the priest. Father Pat was a great talker, and sitting by the little fire in the parlour he spoke to him not only of Horace and Virgil, but of Shakespeare and Milton, the histories of Greece, Rome, and England. And then a good many books, news-papers and magazines found their way from the landlords' houses into the priest's parlour. All these, and especially the newspapers, the boy devoured greedily.

This was in '70, when Ireland was peaceful, and the tenants came trooping in on rent day and paid their rents to a man. The oldest inhabitant could only recall one agrarian murder, and the cutting off the tails of the cattle was a crime unknown.[158] All the servants, butlers, footmen, coachmen, gamekeepers, and bailiffs had been ten, fifteen, or twenty years in their various employments; the labourers too came to and fro daily till they died, and then their places were taken by scarcely less familiar faces. This was at a time when

Ireland was a land of peace, and we loved and reposed so
much trust in each other that we could not believe the news
that Sir A—— had dismissed his favourite bailiff Daly for
stealing, insolence, and drunkenness. Daly, the man we all
knew so well, had he stolen? Daly, whose son James had
been educated under our eyes by the priest? Too true that it
had been rumoured lately that James was misconducting
himself: that he was always in the country town, that he was
often seen talking with the proprietor of a Radical print; that
he read Darwin, had ceased to believe in Christ, and, worst of
all, that he was the writer of some very unpleasant articles
which had lately appeared in the 'Clare Telegraph.'[159] We did
not wish to believe ill of James, and we avoided as much as
possible speaking of his Darwinism and his friendship with the
editor, etc. But we were, alas! soon forced to admit that these
rumours were not without foundation, for next week an article
appeared in the 'Telegraph,' denouncing Sir A—— as a rack-
renter and an exterminator of the people. There was at first
some doubt as to the authorship of this article, but James,
whom we had petted and spoilt, now threw off the mask; and
going from public-house to public-house, feeding on flattery,
his vanity and his patriotism grew together. For a moment it
seemed as if James would degenerate into a common, drunken,
village ruffian; but there was more than that in James, and he
soon began to see that Ireland was still a country where you
would have to do something besides talking to get a living.
There is no way of earning a livelihood except by farming,
and there is only one kind of farming that is profitable—and
that is to fatten cattle. Nothing can be simpler. You hire a
farm, say a hundred acres of pasture land; you buy yearling
bullocks at the nearest fair, you allow them to eat the grass for
some months, and then you drive them to another fair and
sell them. If the price of cattle goes up, you make money; if it
goes down, you lose money. Of course a certain skill is required
to choose the cattle that are likely to fatten best, but that is soon
acquired; and if it can't be acquired the herdsman supplies the
requisite judgement. But James did not require any herdsman

to point out to him the difference between good and bad bullocks; he had lived all his life among them, and he knew the beasts that were likely to suit him. And for three years he attended the fairs buying and selling cattle, making his way steadily upwards; but, notwithstanding his good fortune, he did not cease to speak on all occasions of his country's wrongs. In the afternoon he was always at the railway station with a newspaper under his arm, in the evening in the bar-room of the hotel, and in 1877[160] when the failure of the potato crop threatened famine, and Davitt and Parnell came down to Mayo to start the Land League, James was at once appointed president of the local branch.[161] Then he did not cease to call landlords land-thieves in the 'Telegraph,' and he became the special correspondent of the 'Freeman's Journal', and supplied that excellent journal with much information concerning the distress prevailing in the West. In a few months he was removed to the head of the League in Dublin, where he continued to work to obtain his country's freedom, until he was thrown into prison under Mr. Forster's Act: and once an Irishman has been in prison for a political offence—and in Ireland anything and everything is a political offence—he becomes at once an immortal.

James, on his release from prison, was of course elected Member of Parliament;[162] a few questions were asked as to what he would live on, and the usual answer was given—journalism.

Imagine, therefore, this Celtic peasant—for James is a pure unadulterated peasant; chance had given him an intelligence a little sharper than his cousins who remain in the Western bogs, but he is of the soil as they are; he is cunning, selfish, cruel, even as they; his blood is thin with centuries of poverty, damp hovels, potatoes, servility; his passions are dull and sullen as an instinct. And this half-animal walks out of Euston Square[163] into London. He is dazzled, bewildered, and a little cowed; he steals out of the splendour and turmoil to his lodging in Lambeth.[164] He cannot realise the city yet, all is vague, uncertain; but the low peasant nature ferments, and foul imaginings of gross gratifications bubble and burst in the brain.[165] He knows the women who pass are *demi-monde*, though they appear like houris in some Mahomedan paradise; they are so wonderfully dressed, so beautiful, so bewitching.[166] The long colonnade of Regent Street turns round against the pale blue sky, the telegraph wires come out distinct on the rose tints. The evening is breathless; the street is swept clean as a ballroom; the pungent odour of the cigarette rises, and from the cloaks of the women passing are wafted whiffs of patchouli; women look exquisite in white fur and silk come down the steps of a restaurant, while their companions, tall young Englishmen, with fashionable capes hanging from their broad shoulders, and pale aristocratic faces, escort them. The poor savage Celt steps out of the atmosphere of a flower shop, the strong perfume of the gardenias, the fine wine-like fragrance of the roses sickens him, for his nostrils are filled with the rank smells of the dung-heap, the pig, the damp cabin, the dirty paraffin-oil odour of the West. His brain is shaken, his throat is dry, and with a feeling akin to nausea his heart seems to come up to his mouth; his eyes grow dim; but he revolts against it; he turns like a dog from a vanille ice, he turns from all this glitter and refinement of passion—as well strive to feed a hyena on chocolate creams; a plainer, coarser food is what he longs for; he is savage with envy and rage; he cannot seize any fragment of this scintillating elusive life that passes him; he dare not yet aspire to be one of that gay throng.[167] And that terrible thick brogue—how ashamed he is of it. He strives to bite off the end as he speaks in the vapoury, greasy eating-house at the end of his street. There he can devour beef and pudding and drink of beer till he is heavy and torpid with undigested food; he can take home a bottle of whisky and drink himself drunk. The plain satisfaction of his instincts is to this peasant a mighty joy; all the centuries of fasting find a vent in these cheap orgies and patriotism is apotheosised in pudding. He looks forward to night, and he counts the hours of the afternoon, and, standing on the grating outside he exhales the odours, excites his eyes, and lashes his appetite with the thong of anticipation.[168]

The House is sitting. The Irish Members are talking of some Bill of vital importance. One after another they get up, maddeningly irrelevant are their remarks, hideous is their English.[169] It is James Daly's turn to speak. He looks at the clock, half-past one. Heavens! the streets will be empty when the House breaks up.[170] His thoughts are far away from Ireland and her wrongs.[171] He would give his life to get away, but the eyes of Parnell are upon him, and he mumbles along with his rattletrap sentences grown lame in longing and disconnected in despair.

James Daly is one of the numerous servitude that Parnell has enlisted and that America supports. In Clare he seemed to have some little ability, but in the House of Commons his platitude is painfully apparent, and from his vulgarities the leaders of his party shrink. Still he is malleably facile, quick to observe and correct his deficiencies, and in two or three years the most obvious marking of the peasant origin will be rubbed away. The thick, greasy brogue will remain, the soul of the soil, of the bog, will still be reflected in his face, but when he has edged his way into some Bayswater drawing-room you will be surprised at how quietly he speaks and the tact he shows. And his tastes have refined. He has learned to despise the cheap eating-house,[172] he frequents fashionable restaurants, sips champagne and chats fluently with the actresses. What will eventually become of him? Will he go back to Ireland and continue cattle-farming? No. He will either marry a girl with money, or he will go to America and lecture to the pot-boys and housemaids on the wrongs of the old country, or he will continue to live mysteriously in London—how, nobody can tell. On the subject of the landlords' incomes the Parnellites are glib enough: concerning their own they are mute. There is, of course, a great deal of talk about journalism, but in the case of those who cannot even write a letter intelligently, much less an article, other expedients are resorted to. The most common of these is to fill half a dozen wash-tubs with chemicals, and when a friend calls to turn a handle and ask him to notice the bubbles that rise to the top and then . . . inventions . . .

patents, etc., for there is no sorer subject with these political parasites than to suggest that they live on the nursemaids in America.[173] But in the midst of all this lying there is a truth to be recognised—these Irishmen love their country. The Parnellite party is to-day so strongly knit, but to-morrow it may be bankrupt, or it may wax stronger and mightier and force England to surrender; one solution is as likely as another, but in either eventuality James Daly's love of Ireland will remain the same as it was when he advised the peasant lads in the West to boycott and not to murder Ferick. Life will make him humble, and when he has settled down, when he has children about him, he will begin to grow conscious of the fact that the weak must submit to the strong; that some are born to live in obscurity, others in glory. He will have learned that he personally is not great nor noble, but he will never learn that his country is neither great nor noble. He may even betray his country by accepting some government appointment, but he will never cease to believe in her, to laud and to love her. I am a close observer of life, and I am, I think, as free from prejudice as any man, but this I am bound to admit—that it is impossible to over-estimate the patriotism of Irishmen, '*L'amour de l'Irlande est chez eux comme un vice de constitution que rien ne peut ni pourra jamais déraciner:*' Their love of Ireland is, as it were, a sort of constitutional vice that nothing can, that nothing will be able to uproot.

A CASTLE OF YESTERDAY.[174]

To awake in the vague, cold darkness; to awake with the brain filled with all the hallucinations of midnight—I am in a large four-posted bed . . . the room, yes, I know it all, but how cold are the white curtains of the bed, and the windows are draped in white, and how strange is the shadowy servant moving about with the candle that burns, oh, so brightly, in the cold dark! There is something of a funeral in the room, and I am pained with a blurred and confused, but none the less a very real, impression of illness, of death.

'It is nearly five o'clock, sir, and Mr. Dacre said he would be here about that time; it won't do to keep him waiting.'

The dreams are torn and fall into the void of night, and again I grow alive to the realities of the hour. Of course, how stupid of me I had forgotten, but now I remember, I am going out duck-shooting with my friend Dacre; he sent the boat in a cart overnight, and I sent it on a couple of miles up the lake, and we shall drive there, and then we will row out a mile or so to a point that lies—I think he told me somewhere near Castle Burk———[175] But here my retrospect is interrupted by the grating of wheels on the gravel and a loud whistling. 'Open the window,' I cry, 'and tell him I shall be down in five minutes.'

A rush of cold air that causes me to disappear under the bedclothes, but even there I hear a loud young voice speaking as if out of the heart of the night.

'Down in *five* minutes? I'll see he is down in *one* minute; tell him I am coming upstairs.'

A few moments after a loud trampling of feet comes resounding along the corridor, and a tall, dark, well-built young man strides into the room. He is dressed in knickerbockers and a Norfolk jacket; a thick comforter is wound round his throat.

'Now then, lift your leg, shake your leg,' he cries, laughing uproariously the while, 'we haven't a moment to lose, it is on the stroke of five; we have three miles to drive and a mile to row, and if we aren't there before daylight it is all up with us. Now, then, do make haste. No bath, no shaving, no breakfast. Take a hunch of bread if you like. Now then, pull on your clothes; you'll wash yourself when you come home, or perhaps we'll get as much washing as we want in the lake, for it is blowing pretty strong, I can tell you.'

'I hope you didn't forget to load some cartridges with number two shot last night, and some with number four?'

'That's all right, I have fifty cartridges in the bag; if we fire all that away we won't do bad, I guess. But do be quick and lace up those boots.'

Soon after we are on the car. The horse trots briskly. It is not very dark, but the sky, how grey it is, and how cold the wind is! We draw the rugs around our feet and discuss the prospects of sport. There will be no mistake about the boat, none; it was left in charge of the shepherd; we have only to knock at the door, he'll be up in a moment, he will take care of the horse and help us to launch the boat. Then we lapse into silence, and each lays plans to outdo the other. The horse trots into a village. There is the priest's house; see its white walls and green door; see the grey gaunt chapel and its tombstones. Facing them there are some hovels; one is licensed to sell spirits and tobacco, another has fallen and only a fragment of roof covers the sleepers; and a little farther on there is a cottage that looks cleaner and more respectable, and there is a forge at the corner of the road. Thinking of the ducks I talk to Dacre about his farming. He declares that things are going from bad to worse, and that if there is not a rise in the price of cattle he will be bankrupt. He did not sell his bullocks last October because the price was so bad, but he will not be able to keep them beyond May; go they must. Dacre is a young Scotchman who came to settle in Mayo some eight or nine years ago. The Scotch farmer is a characteristic of Ireland. Here and there you find these strong, thrifty Northern men, forming, with their neat farmyards and their richly ploughed fields, a striking contrast to the desolate hillsides which the peasants scratch rather than till with wretched spades and hoes. But Ireland is a country of failure and ruin, nothing succeeds there but patriotism, and after a few years of trial even the hard-working Scotchmen left in despair. Some few remained, and, surrendering gradually their civilised agriculture, sought to win back some part of their lost fortune in adopting the aboriginal and native cattle-rearing. Mr. Dacre is one of these. He farms three hundred acres of land, keeps a subscription pack of harriers, and is the best rider and the best shot in the county. A strong handsome young man whose life is passed in the saddle or on the moor with his gun; jovial and genial he is, and we laugh heartily as we tell the tale of a girl or recall a sporting reminiscence. The horse trots briskly, the country is veiled in shadow, the cattle are sleeping in the fields, and as we pass out of the night of some overhanging trees we come in sight of the stormy lake.[176]

'This is the place,' says Dacre, pulling up in front of a hut by the roadside, 'do you get out the guns and I'll go and wake the fellow up.'

The flaring peat-fire, with tongues of red flame darting into the darkness, and the heaps of white ash; the sheep-dog is sleeping, his fine nose is thrown up as we approach the door, and barking violently he challenges our entrance.

'All right, your honour,' cries a voice out of the darkness, and struggling into a pair of trousers a man appears. He warms his hands, and a moment after he is with us helping to take the horse out of the car, and as he leads him into the hut, and ties him up by the fireside, he tells us that we shall find the boat on the shore. We shoulder the oars, and the peasant comes down to help us to get afloat. A wild wind is blowing; the headlands are but vague shadows seen like clouds upon the grey sky, and the dim expanse of water breaks into waves, whose crests are treacherously white.[177] And the boat that looked so large in the cart last night now seems the veriest cockle-shell. The peasant notices this, and he speaks about the lake being a little rough. But we do not listen: I seize the bow oar, Dacre takes the stroke, and kicks the spaniel into his place in the stern, and we are shoved into deep water. Now pull away! But the boat is like lead, and it seems almost impossible to force her through the waves: heavy waves are breaking sharply about us, and oars are buried in them. Our arms are strong, our will is as iron, and we get half a mile from the shore; we round the headland and the dark lake is all about us,—unutterably dark and chill. Our difficulties now increase tenfold, our little boat can hardly rise above the wallowing waves, and the oars are buried deeper than ever. On our right are the vast ruins of a feudal castle, before us there is nothing but the lake. Pull, pull, but the boat makes but little way, and the spaniel is jumping about, striving to avoid the waves.

I hear them as they splash against the bow, as they fall about my back. Then the chill of water strikes through my big shooting boots. I look down, but it is so dark I can scarcely see.

'There seems to be a lot of water in this boat, Dacre.'

'Nonsense,' he replies, 'row on; if we don't get there before daybreak we are done; the ducks coming from their feeding-ground alight there at daybreak, and they remain a few minutes pecking and pluming their feathers: row on.'

It seems to me impossible it could be right for so much water to be in the boat, but yielding to Dacre's superior knowledge of boats, I stick my feet against the seat in front of me, and pull doggedly. The minutes elapse slowly, and again I feel conscious that the water is rising about my legs. I put my hand down; it seems to me that the boat is half full of water.

'I don't care what you say, but it can't be right that the boat should be half full of water. Put down your hand and try.'

'By God, it is up to my elbow! have we anything to bale her with? No, there is a hole in the saucepan . . . Here, give me up your oar and get into the stern, and bale out with your hat . . . that infernal dog will upset us . . . lie down, sir, lie down. My God, there is a lot of water in the boat! I think you had better be getting off your coat and shoes, we'll have to swim for this . . .

'Swim! that's all very well for you, but we're four hundred yards from shore, and I can't swim fifty yards.'

'Then bale, I tell you—bale like mad!'

One glance before I go to work: a dreary expanse of a dark Irish lake, vague shores shadowy as death, a tiny boat full of water. How sharply the thought cuts; a severing with all things, no further progress; projects and friends, all suddenly stand and look at you . . . and what a pity, the novel I am writing will never be finished—never!

'Bale, man, bale!' cries Dacre, as he pulls towards the shore, and hatful after hatful of water is thrown over the side. How awful the lake's loneliness! how strangely tense a moment of peril! a moment or a few minutes have been wondrously prolonged; magically each second has dropped out of the glass of time, and yet it is but physical pain, there is none of the sickening sorrow, the dull, aching despair of men who suffer with life before them empty and vacant, only a thrilling sense of severing, and soon even that is lost in work.[178]

But the boat does not leak, and when her head is turned from the waves she ceases to take in water. But we do not perceive this, and Dacre puts all his strength into one oar for the waves are driven shoreward; I bale fast and furiously; at last the keel grates on the pebbles.

Thank goodness! I was about done for.

'Where are we?'

'At Castle Carra.[179] Get the cartridges out of the boat, I hope they aren't all wet; we may get a duck or two on the off side of the headland.'

'But I am wet through—I don't know if you are—and my hat is——

'Not up to much,' he replied laughing; 'you had better tie your handkerchief round your head. We can't get out of this place till daylight, these rocks are slippery and full of holes, and I would prefer to catch a cold than to risk breaking my leg down one of these infernal crevices.'

As far as I see we are on a neck of land paved as it were with enormous rocks; out of the space, there grows a dense growth of stunted hazel; on the height at the back there are some tall trees, and the ivy-grown ruin is ringed about with bunched bushes. Under these we sit, striving to forget time in the discussion of our narrow escape.[180] But the moon passes out of the trailing wrack into a clear space of sky, and dawn seems far away. Then to escape the bitter bleakness of the wind we propose, now that there is a little light, to get into the shelter of the roofless castle. Dacre says he'll be able to find the way, and after much scratching amid the bushes, and one cruel fall on the rocks, we reach some grass-grown steps and climb through an aperture into what was once probably the great hall. A high gable shows black and massy against the sky, and tall grass and weeds grow about our feet, and farther away the arching has fallen and forms a sort of pathway to the vault beneath. Centuries of ivy are on the walls, and their surfaces are broken by wide fissures, vague and undistinguishable in the shadow and the cold gloom. But as the moon brightens I see, some fifteen feet above me, a staircase—a secret staircase ascending through the enormous thickness of the walls. What were these strange ways used for? who were they who trod them centuries ago? Slender women in clinging and trailing garments, bearded chieftains, their iron heels clanging; and as I evoke the past, rich fancies come to me, and the nostalgia of those distant days, strong days that were better and happier than ours, comes upon me swiftly, as a bitter poison pulsing in blood and brain; and regardless of my friend's counsels, I climb towards the strange stairway, as if I would pass backwards out of this fitful and febrile age to one bigger and healthier and simpler. These walls have been touched by hands that trembled not as mine, and I shall never touch those hands, and the eyes that looked down through this loophole on wild foes will never be known to mine. Ah! I should have known those men, should have fought out my life with them, and not grown sick with grief in this querulous age. And those women of early Ireland I should have seen holding their robes from their feet as they ascended this stair to the battlements, to watch for their husbands and brothers coming back fresh from border forays with beeves and prisoners . . .

And when amid the beeves and prisoners they saw a stretcher whereon the wounded or dead man was laid, they sat on these very steps where I am standing, and wept. And when the castle was besieged they fled down the passage through the gable through which I am now passing. The stair descends to an embrasure in the wall, and the moonlight is streaming through, and there is something there—a soft low snoring in the moonlight; the staircase descends before me, but I cannot follow it, I cannot pass this ghostly ray of moonlight.[181]

And then the thing ceases to snore in the moonlight, and a white form passes softly down that length of stair, softly away; and then the large and beautifully soft white form comes back, comes up softly, so softly towards the moonlight and me. That moon ray is not so chill as I, and this bloodless agony is more terrible than mortal death. Death that is darkness were sweet, but this cold white spirit of death dreadful to behold; this icy death of wandering white is a terrible death to be taken in.[182]

And where has it passed to, is it about me, will it come back to me again? There is sweat upon my brow, there is death in my heart. Full of the wild water's tune the gaunt castle[183] rises; the secret ways curl up to the savage ivy, and the sky is ghostly pale. Oh, the lapsing tune of the lake! oh, the masses of stone, damp and smooth with the dews of a thousand years! Sickness and terror to look back, terror in the neck and shoulders, like a spirit escaping through a shadowland, I grope my way down these ancient walls.

.　.　.　.　.

I hear a voice calling in the hall below; my heart bounds to the living world. But not at once do I dare make answer,[184] and trembling I make my way to the aperture whence I came. Time seems to have stood still since I left Dacre sitting with his spaniel amid the weed-grown banqueting hall, and I have to ask him to help me down. The place is still ghostly and strange in the grey dawn, but it is natural and homely compared with the minutes of torture I have suffered up in those ancient walls, wet and smooth with age.

'What is the matter with you—you seem frightened out of your life?'

'No, I am only a little cold—wet and cold.'

'Well, then, look alive, I think day is about to break. Let's make haste and get down to the corner before the ducks come in.'

Night gathers her blue garments about her, and the yellow skirt of dawn appears above the mountains, but it is not yet day, and as we scramble through the rocks and bushes, a strange white form swoops through the twilight. Dacre fired, and, through what seemed a sudden shower of snow, a great snowy owl falls at our feet. This, then, was the spirit of the castle whom I had heard snoring in the wintry moonlight.

'I am sorry. The great snowy owl is almost extinct; a couple have been known to frequent the castle for years.'

As we made our way through the castle gateway, we saw the traces of the moat that once divided the neck of the land and completed the isolation of the castle. It once covered the entire promontory. The ruins of the outlying fortifications extend to the edge of the lake: a barbaric chieftain and a numerous servitude once lived there: and now far down the shores of the lake the *silhouette* of another castle appears through the lingering twilight, and on the island far away there still stands a corner wall.[185] Ireland, land of brown bog and fabulous ruin! On every commanding height, generally on a wild promontory harassed by the waves of these tideless inland seas, we find remains of the castles of Irish chieftains—remains full of penetrating poetry, and silent suggestion of turbulent life and the glitter of battle. We dream of border forays and cattle-lifting, but all is vague, and of the inner economy of these tribal people we know less than of the Babylonians or the ancient Egyptians. That they once were is all we know. And now, passing to the mainland, I find the ruins of what is almost a modern house; there is a vast courtyard, and in the centre a colossal stone fox, and farther away is the ruin of the great gateway, and on the hill stand colossal foxhounds. It was here that the descendants of the castle's chieftains came on the decline of brigandage; it was here that they drank, swore, hunted, and fought duels at twelve paces.

A CASTLE OF TO-DAY.[186]

A few days after our return from the north-west, my host said, throwing a letter across the table:

'This is from Lady Ardilaun, a neighbour of mine, asking us on a visit to Ashford.'[187]

All who do not live more than ten or twelve miles apart are next-door neighbours in Ireland, and as the jolting-car pursued its way along the interminable roads, my friend told me all he knew of the people we were going to stay with.[188] Lord Ardilaun is a man of immense wealth. It is said that he sold his share in the great brewery (Guinness's brewery) for a million of money.[189] This money he has invested in different securities all over the world; his landed property, although large, is only a small part of his income; he is the only man in Ireland who is in a position to defy the Land League. Hence his unpopularity.

'Is he unpopular?'

'For the moment; and it is a shame that it should be so, for no man ever lived who behaved more generously to Ireland than he. Others may be accused of drawing money from Ireland, and spending it on the banks of the Thames and the Seine, but not he. When he was a member for Dublin, he bought Stephen's Green; it was then a savage waste; he spent thousands of pounds planting trees, making artificial water, and inclosing it, and presented it to the city. He bought the Rotunda, made it into a beautiful winter garden, where the people might go of an evening, walk and listen to the band playing.[190] At first everybody thought it delightful; but sooner or later, like everything else in Ireland, it was sneered at, and when the people finally refused to go near it, it was sold. Lord Ardilaun was then member for Dublin, and at the next general election he was beaten. And the same want of sympathy is shown to him at Ashford. Would you believe it, he is guarded by policemen in a place where he has spent thousands and thousands of pounds, where he has done more real good—that is to say, good in the sense of encouraging industry, good in the sense of relieving suffering—than perhaps any Irishman that ever lived? At the present moment I hear that his labour bill is over two hundred a week. Any other man who had been requited as he has been would have left the country long ago; but when people are naturally good, they go on being good in spite of all opposition.'[191]

'Then how do you account for his unpopularity?'

'First his large fortune enabled him to successfully resist the Land League, secondly he is a Protestant, and thirdly he is a Conservative. In Ireland popularity is bought with hatred of England; if you are a Catholic so much the better—indeed it is a distinct advantage to be a Catholic, but the first of all things is to hate England.'

While speaking we grow gradually conscious of certain changes in the aspect of the country: it seems more orderly, and it wears an air of well-to-do-ness that we had not before observed. The rickety walls built out of loose round stones piled one on top of the other have disappeared and are replaced by handsome stone and mortar walls; and the cottages of the peasants are less dirty, and here and there the landscape is marked by small cleanly-built slated houses. Upon questioning our driver we learn that we are now entering upon Lord Ardilaun's estate, and as the panting horse drags the car to the top of a high hill he says, 'That's Lough Corrib, the largest lake but one in Ireland; thirty miles long by ten wide.' And the view as it now appears over the verge of the long line of sloping green sward is full of an august and visionary beauty. Below us, falling in sweet inclining plain, a sea of green turf flows in and out of stone walls and occasional clumps of trees down to the rocky promontories, the reedy reaches and the long curved woods which sweep about the castle—such a castle as Gautier[192] would have loved to describe—that Lord Ardilaun has built on this beautiful Irish land. There it stands on that green headland with the billows of a tideless sea, lashing about its base; and oh! the towers and battlements rising out of the bending foliage of ten thousand trees. The lake from where we stand looks like a girdle of pale grey silk bound about the green garments of the Emerald Isle: the long line of mountains upbreaking in jagged outlines, through a drift of clouds—now dark with storm, now resplendent with sunshine! And we lift the unsatiated eyes from this rapture of scenical loveliness.

We are still two miles from our destination, and as we advance signs of wealth and industry increase. We pass large roads, domain walls in process of construction, and a large archway upon which at least a hundred men are at work. And as I gaze I ponder on the crookedness of the Celtic mind; it[193] would put an end to all I see around me, and would willingly relapse into dirt and patriotism—which are apparently but two words for one and the same thing. On either side of us the park now spreads. Through the hillocks hundreds and hundreds of fallow deer move away at our approach, and over the crest of a hill the broad bluff red-deer raise their antlered heads and gaze at us as steadfastly as lions. From the deer-park we go into the drawing-room-like beauties of the pleasure-grounds, and skirting by the laurel-filled nooks and rhododendron-covered slopes, overhung by the dark branches of cedars, we find ourselves facing the river, and it is only after some little difficulty that our horse is induced to trust himself on the picturesque wooden-way which in drawbridge fashion spans the inky stream which whirls round the point on its way to the lake.

Those who love life welcome new impulses, and desire the emotion of unexpected impressions. I am such a one; and the simple pleasure of sitting at a farm window, watching the villagers strolling in bands and couples and single figures across the darkening green, listening to the chattering voices of loitering women, to the howl of a distant dog, to all the vague sounds and shadows that mark the sinking to rest of the world, have never failed to thrill my heart with happiness. 'The poetry of the world is never dead,' and to me it is now an exquisite delight as I stand in long shadowy saloon brushing my hair for dinner to see the moon[194] shining on a vast lake, to watch the weird darkness of the buttresses and the romantic enchantment of the battlements, now standing out sharp against a silvery cloud, from which the moon slowly passes— as Shelley would say,

> like a dying lady, lean and pale,
> Who totters forth, wrapt in a gauzy veil,
> Out of her chamber, led by the insane
> And feeble wanderings of her fading brain.[195]

And after a week spent in the thin, mean poverty of the north-west, amid the sadness of ruined things, this strangely beautiful castle renders me singularly happy. The sight of the long drawing-room, full of refined faces glowing upon the warm shadows, and lights of the shaded lamps, comes with a sense of welcome relief. And to awake in the cool spaces of a bedroom, beautiful and bright with Indian curtains, and musical with the rippling sound of the lake's billow, is also full of gracious charm and delicate suggestion of poetry to him who is alive to the artistic requirements of to-day. And then there are the pleasant morning greetings to look forward to,[196] and the sitting down to breakfast in the oak room within sight of the fountains that foam so lovely and so white upon an endless background of mountain and lake[197]. Here we are almost shut out of the storm and gloom of crime and poverty that enfolds the land, but even here the shadow of murder and outrage falls across our way. For as we sit at breakfast[198] we hear the smothered detonation of the dynamite exploding in the huge moat which our host is having cut through the solid rock, and sometimes[199] small splinters of stone strike the windows. Fifty or sixty men are engaged upon this work; and, after breakfast,[200] as we walk down the grounds, we examine this new fortification, which when finished will separate the castle from the mainland. It is thirty feet deep by twenty feet wide.

'You see,' says our host, 'I have a taste for the picturesque. The moat will be protected by battlements, and cannon will be placed at convenient distances. I shall be able to defend myself in case of invasion, and as the drawbridge will be raised nightly it will be difficult for the dynamiters to get at me.'

But the day I shall remember best of the four days passed in this beautiful western retreat is the last day. It has been arranged that we are to go in the yacht (she now rides at anchor, her steam up, under the castle walls) to picnic on an island some miles down the lake—an island famous for some late pagan and some early Christian ruins.[201] The day is breathless, but the sky is full of a soft grey light; and in the fairy-like silences of the lake, when nothing is heard between the pauses of the conversation but the ripple of the water along the vessel's side, and the subdued panting of the machine, the many aspects of this noble wilderness, the wild outlines of the guardian mountains, the dark promontories covered with rough wood, the marshy shores where the heron stalks, arise as supernaturally and calm as the visions of an Icelandic god, and in the exquisite clarity every detail is visible; the shadows of the pines fall like ink into the smooth mirror. And now the chain rattles through the port-hole, the steamer swings at anchor, and we are helped by the sailors into the small boat. The island, *ma foi*, is a large one—some sixty or seventy acres—and on the side we landed on it is cultivated by three families, and the land has passed from father to son, so it is said, for the last thousand years. In any case the island has never been without its three families—there is the boat in which they transport their farm produce, there are their cottages, there is the grave-yard, and here is the church that St. Patrick's brother (the hermit) built in the fifth century; and the paved path leading from it to his cell is distinctly visible along which he walked fourteen hundred years ago, and along which we walk to-day; and here are the pagan remains, but we cannot look farther back. Behind this stone is the savage darkness out of which we, who now examine this mute record with gloved fingers, slowly and painfully crawled. This island is a little world complete in itself—a little world lost and forgotten in the midst of a greater world. But lost though it be and forgotten, it is strangely present in our minds to-day, and the poetry it evokes is strongly intense and penetrating; and the nostalgia of the past holds me in tether, and I cannot escape it even when quaffing champagne on the tower built for picnicking purposes, nor when looking over Lady Ardilaun's shoulder while she sketches with a free and certain hand a long range of jagged mountains—one of the mountain prospects she loves so dearly, and with which her London drawing-room is so beautifully decorated. The scene is now supernaturally still. The day dies in pale greys and soft pink tints, and harmonies in mauve more delicate and elusive than the most beautiful Japanese water-colour; the lake hangs like a grey veil behind the dark pine-woods through which we wander, making our way to the yacht; and at the vistas we look on the long wavy lines of mountains that enclose the horizon, and they seem now like women sleeping the sleep of enchantment, and the mountains whose precipitous bases rise out of the lake are as fabulous creatures in a northern legend guarding the solitude. Our eyes follow the black flight of the cormorant along the smooth greyness of the water, and our souls are filled and stilled with a sadness that is at one with the knowledge that the dear day we have lived through is now a day that is over and done; and as we think of this lonely island, its ruined church, its grave-yard and the endless generations that lie there, we must fain dream of the lightness of life, of the oblivion that awaits us, of those eternal and simple truths of which even the centuries of barbarous dust lying beneath our feet has in its day dreamed of even as bitterly as we.

On the following day I started for Dublin. The carriage is full of Irish Members and American agitators. They denounce the injustice of England, and proclaim the sweet Irish peace that will follow on Home Rule.

AN EVICTION.

A strange woman lives in the west of Ireland; a sort of she-Nero besotted with drink and maddened with lust of cruelty. She is a woman with pale blue eyes, so pale that they look like porcelain; she is middle-aged, she is fat, she is dressed in man's clothes. Iron-grey hair grows thinly over large scabs of dirt, the red flesh of the cheeks is loose and hanging, and something shapeless moves beneath the long, filthy jacket which falls like a petticoat and is bound about her with a leathern strap; her legs are covered in a pair of corduroy trousers, patched and greased and stained with abominable stains; and the thick, coarse hand, which looks as if it were all thumbs, twitches at the hem of the discoloured jacket.

The judge (to the solicitor): 'You might grant the tenant time if he promises to pay.'

Miss Barrett (in a bellowing, half-drunken tone): 'Certainly not.'

A decree of ejectment is granted.

And the pale blue eyes catch expression horribly indicative of cruelty and rapacity, but only to fade a moment after into the usual helpless semi-idiotic stare. Other cases have to be heard, and Miss Barrett consults with her companion, Miss McCoy, a tall, raw-boned Scotchwoman, so tightly buttoned up in a brown, mud-smeared ulster, that it is difficult to say if her undergarment is a petticoat or a pair of trousers.[202]

The night is falling, and the people are coming out of the court-house. The sullen faces of the peasants are hardly visible in the gloom, but their exclamations of hatred are very audible. 'You dirty old petticoated brandy vessels; oh, the filthy animals!'[203]

But paying no attention to these jeers, the two women pass with their guard of police and their bailiffs to the nearest public-house; and from public-house to public-house they go, drinking and cursing with ever-increasing ardour until at last the glass slips from their hands and the oath dies on their lips, and they fall helpless on the ground. Then they are piled up and tied on a car by the police and driven home to sleep off the effects of their drunken bout.

Many are the legends concerning Miss Barrett. It is said that she was once—a quarter of a century ago—a pretty and graceful Irish girl, whose blue eyes and merry voice were the delight of her friends, and particularly of a young English painter with whom she was passionately in love. It is suggested that he painted her as Ophelia and that the picture still exists in London; but her father, so report goes, would not hear of the marriage and sent his daughter abroad in the charge of a companion A few weeks after he died, and Miss Barrett came travelling back, as fast as express trains could bring her, to bury her father and marry her painter. But the painter had already married another, and Miss Barrett returned to her Western home and spoke of founding a convent.[204] That there is some truth in these stories is probable enough, for it is certain that Miss Barrett was not only born, but once lived, as a lady, but the cause of her decline into the sewer of debauchery is not known, and it is impossible to trace the steps by which she descended into these lowest and most horrible depths. Golden fortune has however always attended her; relative after relative died, leaving her their properties, which they could not now will away from her, and she is now possessed of vast wealth, which she has no power or way of spending except in an occasional drinking-bout with her bailiffs and caretakers in a county town.

Her house and grounds once differed nowise from those of the surrounding gentry; but the same changes have taken place in them as in herself. How dissolute, how degraded! All the trees have been cut down, and the hewn stumps show naked out of the great green field. In large scabs the cement is falling from the wall; the windows are broken and are barricaded on the inside with rough boards. The hall-door is nailed up, and there are great beams of wood and stones lying about; clearly the only entrance used is the back one. Inside there is but filth and barrenness. You can tell which was the drawing-room by the broken piano, by the gilt cornices that strew the floor. A patch of carpet remains, a deal table stands in the middle of the room. Apparently washing was once done here, for a wash-tub stands on a fragile Chippendale chair that somehow escaped destruction before the room was abandoned. In the bedrooms only the huge four-posters remain; foul earthy odours assail your nostrils;[205] damp, decay, and dust meet you alternately and in combination. Bottles and broken glasses grow more frequent as you descend to the kitchen—now the principal apartment of Miss Barrett and her sister-in-arms, Miss McCoy; and there their herdsmen and bailiffs come of an evening and are made riotous with whisky,—and the lampless Irish night grows shrill with shriekings, and the echoes of orgie follow the traveller across the desolate bogs.

The house is surrounded by immense pasture-lands—thousands of acres, from which the tenants have been driven at different times. These are stocked with herds of sheep and cattle. Dressed as a man, in her dreadful corduroy trousers and felt hat, Miss Barrett attends the fairs, and counselled by her herdsmen she buys and sells, spitting and swearing and drinking out of a flask, while she drives the bargain. The sexual economy of animals has no secrets for her; she goes down before the rams are turned into the fold,[206] and it is she who often passes the usual coat of red paint over the animals' bellies. Miss Barrett is delighted as little as she is disgusted by the procreation of beasts; she merely declines to acknowledge the mystery with which we occidentals have surrounded such things, and having chosen to become a herdsman she accepts the duties in all their completeness. Against her virtue not a word has ever been said; she is execrated in the county in which she lives, but it is for drunkenness and cruelty that she is so violently and vehemently abused. To evict her tenants is her one desire, to harass them with summonses for trespass is her sole amusement. She watched them collectively and individually, and when an unfortunate one is a few months in arrear he is at once served with a writ, law costs are run up, every effort is made to render it impossible for him to save himself from ejectment. If by any chance the money should be scraped together and the tenant saved Miss Barrett is woefully disappointed, for she looks forward to an eviction as men did to cock-fights in the old days . . .

.　　.　　.　　.　　.

The streets of a county town[207] are swarming with police, they are driving in on cars from all sides—great, big, brawny fellows clad in black cloth and armed with rifles and sword-bayonets. They come thronging in from all parts of the country: sergeant and constables from Ballina, Ballinrobe, Ballindine, Clarenorris, Kelimach, Louisburg, Newport[208]—in fact from every station in Mayo,[209] for it is not known if the peasantry will risk eviction. Three car-loads of police are now crossing the railway bridge. The station is deserted, the platform is empty, a single grey line stretches to and is lost in the interminable bog. Nearer the town there are a few green fields belonging to a landlord who keeps a dairy farm. Then come some filthy cottages where roofs are falling and pigs run grunting from the horses' hoofs. The road is flowing with mud. Suddenly a pavement and stone houses appear, then the market-place and the court-house, and then the spire of the church; and grey houses follow as untidily as dirty shirts and towels hung out on a line in a back yard. Dark and dingy goods, thick boots and shoes, coarse clothes, etc., are piled up in the shop windows, but nowhere is seen a flower-vase, a balcony, a fantastic gable.

At the cross roads of Logafoil,[210] about a mile distant on the other side of the town, we perceive long lines of police-men, about a hundred in all. They are drawn up in lines, headed by their different officers and commanded by Major Murphy. Surrounded by a special guard the gaunt hungry Scotchwoman,[211] Miss McCoy, gives her arm to Miss Barrett—that strange creature in corduroy trousers strapped round her with a belt; fat and bloated she is with drink, and her blue eyes stare with the vagueness of coming idiocy. But she wakes up a little when the order to march is given, and as she whispers to her friend an expression of atrocious cruelty steals over the faces of the women. On the other side there is her bailiff—a man named Pratt, whom the peasants assail, as we march, with the bitterest reproaches concerning his birth and the applications he had made for the post of hangman.

'At all events I have gentleman's blood in my veins, even if it did not come to me through the marriage-ring, and that is more than any of you can say.'

'The devil a drop, the Colonel disowned you, your ——— [212] of a mother was caught by a policeman one night in a ditch: that's more like it.'

And with such lively passages of wit, varied with sarcastic allusions of a like delicate nature,[213] the tedium of our walk is enlivened. Hundreds of people have assembled, there is some blowing of horns on the hill-side and at first we think the police will have to charge the people. But having been fired upon lately they are frightened, and allow themselves to be driven back with the butt-ends of the rifles, and the little army is posted about the wretched hut from which a human family is to be driven. So horrible is the place that it seems a mockery, a piece of ferocious cynicism to suggest that the possession of it is about to be contested, and that to restore it to its rightful owner an army has to be gathered together. It lies under the potato-field, and the space between bank and wall is a stream of mud and excrement. The incessant rain has rotted the straw of the roof, and at one end it droops ready to slip down at every moment. The weak walls lean this way and that, and their foundations are clearly sinking away into the wet bog. Hard by the dung-heap, in front of the door, where the pig strives to find a place dry enough to lie in, the mud and filth have lapsed into green liquid where some ducks are paddling; under the thatch there is mould and damp, about the door and window-holes blackness and ooze, mud permeates and soaks through every crevice; the place seems like a rat's nest built on the edge of a cesspool. Not a tree is to be seen, not even a bush. There is the brown bog far away, and the flashes of water where lapwings are flying; there are the tumble-down little walls which separate the fields that the peasants scratch rather than till; there is the desolate lake where waves are breaking and rushes are blown in the wild wind. And this chilling landscape is bound with the usual sash of blue mountains.

[214]Only the voice of a child crying is heard. Pratt and a one-armed man, upon whom the peasants continued to shower the strangest abuse, approach and ask for admittance.

'I'll not open it. 'Tis not like the last day, when you boasted you caught the buck in the house.'

'Now, Thomas,' says Pratt, 'the easy way is the best. If you don't open I'll have to force the door.'

'You hang-in-bone dog! You may thank the law, or you wouldn't come this way to my door; I would scatter your brains on the street, you dirty bloodhound and nameless bastard! My father and grandfather were reared here, and you want to put me out of it—a fellow who couldn't tell who was *his* grandfather. When your old mother called you after Colonel Pratt, to try and knock money out of him, he always denied that you had a drop of his blood in you, and you have not, *Billeen Sollagh.*'[215] This speech is received with roars of laughter, and Pratt puts his shoulder to the door, but it does not give way, and paying no heed to the sarcastic suggestion that he might fetch a long ladder and get down the chimney, he seeks about for a stone. Selecting the largest he can find he launches it against the door. There is a cry from the children within, but the door has not given way. The missile is hurled again and again, and when he starts a plank he levels his next throw at the same place; a piece of wood snaps off short; he is invited to put his hand inside, but he wisely refrains. And all the while the children are crying, and the mother utters unceasingly that long wail traditional with the Gaelic people and always used by them in times of mourning; and on the dung-heap and on the road there is jeering; and wild curses are showered on the extraordinary creature—the lumpy, worn-out debauchee, who stands staring vaguely, her bloated face now and then lighting up in an expression of cruelty, her trembling hand twitching nervously at the hem of her abominable dress. At last the door gives way, and Pratt, the one-handed assistant, and a couple of police, force their way into the black den. There is the father, the wife and her six half-naked children. The father, covered only with a pair of trousers, his hairy shoulders showing through the ragged shirt, rushes out like a wild beast to strangle Pratt, but he is seized by the policemen; and the clearing of the house of furniture is commenced—an iron pot, a few plates, three logs of wood that are used as seats, a chair, a cradle, and some straw and rags on which the whole family slept; Miss Barrett looks on with manifest satisfaction. Here are a few remarks snatched as it were out of the crowd: 'McCoy, have you anything in that flask? You ought to give a drop to your neighbours. Barrett, you buy this old cradle, it was a very lucky one! Who knows what might turn up for you yet, in the shape of some old devil of a husband as ugly as yourself but not so great a drunkard?'

Then the family has to follow the furniture. The father struggles, held fast by two policemen, the children are soon shoved out of the door, but the woman offers a stubborn resistance. She is a strong, stout, shapeless creature. A red petticoat falls to her knees, a shawl is wrapped round her shoulders, and she carries a baby in her arms.

'Ah, you dirty illegitimate beast, I dare you to lay a hand on me; I am an honest woman and not a dirty slut like your mother . . . Don't touch me! Will you? you are breaking my back . . . You are killing the innocent child. Leave go of me! Is there no one here to save me?'

'Now you had better go for the asking; we don't want to hurt you, but out you must go.'

'You don't want to hurt me? I tell ye you are breaking my back. The death of the child be on your head; he isn't a dirty bastard like you. Will you leave me go?'

Pratt pushes her from behind, the one-armed man pulls her

in front, but she always manages to evade the door-way. It is
a marvel how she jerks up the child when it seems on the
point of slipping from her. The woman writhes to and fro; she
shrieks and shrieks again, the red petticoat is twisted round her
waist, and she appears, as she struggles across the doorway in
strong and savage nakedness.

But her strength is beginning to fail her, and at last, uttering
a wild cry, she slips on the ground, screaming that Pratt has
kicked her in the stomach, that she is dying. Leaving his shirt
in the hands of the police the husband slips out of their grasp
and he would have probably done for Pratt had he not been
again seized.

Howls and execrations! Pratt swears he never touched her;
the husband swears he saw him; the one-armed man calls
God to witness to a number of things; and Major Murphy
orders his men to disperse the crowd. Then many things
happen: Miss Barrett loses her brandy-flask, a neighbour
brings in a saucepan of milk,[216] and the wounded woman is
consoled and questioned.

'And where did he kick you, awornine?'[217]

'[218]I'm loth to tell you with all the people about.'

It is infinitely pitiful and infinitely grotesque. The woman,
no doubt, hit herself in her conflict with the bailiff, but she is
evidently pretending to worse injuries than she received. For
her wailing is more horrible than natural; and the suffering of
the little children crying on the dung-heap is more heart-
rending. An hour and a half passes. At last she allows herself
to be helped out of the house, and she is laid down on some
straw under a wall. It seems as if it never could end. The husband goes from group to group collecting evidence against
Pratt; the wife shrieks she is bleeding to death—'that she can
feel it running down her inside'—and the little boys mock at
Miss Barrett's breeches, taunt her with her drunkenness, and
Pratt with his bastardy. At last the doctor arrives. But how is
he to examine her? Those who after so much trouble have
possessed themselves of her house refuse to readmit her even
for a few minutes on any pretext whatever. The woman

writhes on the straw, her red petticoat twisted about her naked red legs; and Pratt, still swearing that he never laid a hand or a foot on her, suggests that the Major should clear away the crowd so that the doctor might examine her at once.

'The woman is not a sheep or a cow and cannot be examined in the open air . . .'

'He is thinking of his old mother, your honour; many a time she was examined in the open air; and more is the pity the wall did not tumble upon her and the Colonel, and we wouldn't have him here—Billy, the bad begot!'

Meanwhile a large hole is being made in the roof, the rafters are being torn up, and the woman in breeches and pot-hat, who it is said was once in love with a painter and sat for a picture of Ophelia, puts a padlock on the door.

A HUNTING BREAKFAST.

'Hallo! Down already? Fall to—what will you have? Here are some beefsteaks and kidneys; you'll find a cold chicken on the sideboard; or will you have a couple of boiled eggs?'

'Thanks, I'll help myself to some chicken and ham, and do you pour me out a cup of coffee.'

'All right, but don't dawdle, there's a good fellow; remember we have a good ten miles to ride.'

'The others aren't down yet; we have lots of time, it isn't nine o'clock.'

'Lynch—is *he* up? What is he doing? Did you look into his room?'

'Yes, he was trying to tie a necktie. I told him to hurry and he said he would not be long.'

'Is the coffee to your liking?'

'Yes, first-rate; I think I'll change my mind and trouble you for a kidney. . . . Thanks, that will do!'

'Ten minutes past nine, and Sally isn't down yet; goodness me—this is so provoking! I must send up to hurry her.'

'You needn't bother; I met the maid in the passage, and she told me Miss Sally was nearly dressed, and would be down in a few minutes. Give me another cup of coffeee . . . What a fellow you are! and for all the hunting we shall have——

'Why, do you really think the hounds will be stopped?'[219]

'So they say. I hear that all the county round Tuam[220] is placarded with notices calling on the farmers to refuse to allow hounds or horses to cross their lands, in consequence of the refusal of the landlords to give twenty per cent. reduction. They say all the coverts are poisoned, and that at an attempt to run a fox the farmers will assemble in hundreds and stone the hounds from the scent—and us too, for the matter of that.'

'God, I should like to see one of the dirty ruffians throw a stone at me! I'd ride at him and flay him within an inch of his life. Hallo! Down at last, Sally? we must be off in a few minutes . . .'

'I assure you, Miss O'Neil, he has not ceased to speak of the time since I came down, and I was down at half-past eight.'

'Oh, he is always like that; I don't mind him now; but where is Mrs. Molloy? Isn't she down yet?

'No, mother sent word that we weren't to wait for her.'

'What are you riding, Miss O'Neil?'

'A young chestnut Mr. Trench was kind enough to lend me. I have no horses of my own: I depend upon the kindness of my friends.'

'But of course they are only too glad to have their horses ridden by so good a rider as you, Miss O'Neil . . . I have heard of you in Leicestershire. I hear that we have no one who could touch you—that if you were to come over, you'd tail us all off.'

'Oh, not at all! I am sure I never should be able to cross your double post and rails . . . I sha'n't be able to ride at all to-day from nervousness, if you are going to watch me.'

'Will you have an egg, Sally? Are you ready for some more coffee?'

'Thanks, I haven't finished this yet . . . but tell me, is it really a fact that the covers are poisoned, and that we shall be stoned if we attempt to run a fox?'

'Impossible to say. Hartley, who came from Tuam last night, says the country is posted with notices?'

'Aren't you afraid, Miss O'Neil? It does seem so odd to one coming from England to hear of poisoned covers and hounds being stoned. I thought the Irish were better sportsmen.'

'Until Parnell and Davitt came with their Land League there wasn't a more sporting peasantry in the world than the Irish, but everybody who has anything to spend has been driven out of the country . . . The Empress of Austria isn't coming to Meath this year on account of the Land League—there's thousands of pounds gone out of the country.'[221]

'And if they don't let the hounds hunt, what shall we do?'

'Nothing for it but to come back again the same way we went . . . We lunch at Mrs. Jack's—she is one of the characters of the County of Galway.'[222]

'Yes, she's got an heiress staying with her; she is the girl's guardian. Now there's your chance, Fleming: but it will take you all your time to outwit the old girl. She'll be down on you like a thousand of bricks if she even suspects you of making up to the girl.'

'Why! Does she not want the girl to marry?'

'Not she; if the girl, Maggie Jordan, does not marry, all the money will go to Mrs Jack's relations. She is an orphan, and the whole family watch her like a lot of hawks. The aunt is ready to fly at any would-be suitor, and Maggie is locked up for days in her room if she so much as dares to look at a man twice . . . The whole thing is very sad.'223

'But who is Mrs. Jack? What is she? Surely a creature like that is not received in society?'

'She was once a great gaunt ugly girl, six feet high, and as strong as a policeman. She had scarcely enough to eat at home, and when she was introduced to a man at a ball, the first thing she said was, "Take me to the supper room," and there she remained gorging as long as he would stop with her, and then she put cakes in her pockets to eat in the carriage going home. But her ball-going was not of long duration; her mother soon found that she was hopeless, and Betsey remained an old maid till she was fifty. Then she married Jack Thorne, a pawnbroker, a county usurer who built a villa residence for her and left her all his money. He was a funny old chap, a brown wig and a splendid set of false teeth. The teeth were much admired by Mrs. Jack; she insisted on his getting them before his marriage, and when he died she did not forget them. She rushed at the coffin, crying, "They are going to bury him in his teeth." Pushing in her fingers, she pulled out one set, wiped them in her handkerchief, and then made another dive after the upper jaw . . . She bought her mother's mourning before the old lady was dead; she had a whole drawerful of clothes, and she used to show them to her friends, and hoped that the fashions would not change before "poor mother passes away." When her brother died she would not let the remains be taken into his own house, and he had to be buried from a lodging.'

'And this is the person with whom we are going to lunch after we have been well stoned by the Land Leaguers! . . . I sha'n't go.'

'Yes, you will; I wouldn't for the world that you should miss seeing Mrs. Jack: and you must really go in for mashing[224] the niece. It will be splendid fun: for Mrs. Jack hasn't the slightest notion of behaving herself. Once I was dining there and got into a dispute with her butler, and the man gave her warning before the entire company.'

'And you say her niece, an heiress, lives with this ignorant, coarse woman?'

'Yes, there are many sad things in life, and this is not the least sad. I assure you the girl is very nice, and to see her brought up alone with this savage creature, never a sweeting influence, never the gleam of light cast by a refining thought, nothing to break the darkness of an animal existence. 'Pon my word it is very sad; to-day the girl is hopeful and pleasant; she is young, but in a few years life will be crushed out of her, and she will be as degraded, and as dead to all the tendernesses of life as that vulgar brute who bought her mourning before her mother was dead.'

'Here you are at last, we can't wait for you; we had better make a start at once, what do you say? Sally, are you ready?'

'I am quite ready; and I think we had better be off . . . What kept you so long Mr. Lynch?'

'Oh! I don't know; sometimes everything seems to go wrong. I could not find my razor-strop, and I could not get my boots on, and I forgot to unpack my new coat last night, and it was in a portmanteau that they had forgotten to bring upstairs. What do you think of the coat? Does it fit all right?'

'For God's sake drink a cup of coffee, and let us get off!'

'Now don't excite yourself, old man. Ring and order the nags round. I shall put a sandwich in my pocket.'

'The scene is a breakfast-room. A silver urn hisses on the table, and over the cups and plates there floats a decided odour of coffee and kidneys. The speakers are Molloy—a tall, strong, fine-looking man, some six feet high; Fleming—a young man, thin and pale, with pale English hair and blue eyes; Lynch—a stout-set man with a heavy jaw and rough hands; Miss O'Neil, or Sally, as she is generally called—a little woman with light yellow hair, small features, tiny feet that move prettily beneath her short riding-habit of green cloth. The men are all dressed in breeches and red coats. Presently they adjourn to the stables, where the hacks are waiting that will carry them to the meet; the hunters have been sent on overnight, and are now munching the corn at a house ten Irish miles distant (twenty kilomètres). The horses canter briskly; there is no time to lose. At the cross roads they meet Rose, Sally's sister, and Mrs. Manly, a lady who has a child every year, rides to hounds three days a week, and is said to have jumped five feet four months before the birth of her last. She joins her admirer, Mr. Molloy, the two sisters ride on in front, and Mr. Lynch tells Mr. Fleming a great deal concerning the respective horsemanship of Rose and Sally. It is difficult to say which is the better. Rose's is a more determined and more bullying method; she takes the horse by the head and holds him as if he were in a vice, pushes him along by main force; whereas Sally is quiet and clever, the horse scarcely feels her light hands. She wants no one to tell her what line to take, she decides immediately and very often squanders[225] the whole field.

It is a misty morning, and out of the greyness the red horsemen come from the right and left. They exchange with us a hasty salutation and press forward. A little farther on we meet the master of the hounds, his splendid pack about his horse's heels, and his two whips[226] trotting behind him. Ominous rumours have reached him that the peasants are determined to stop the hunting, and Mr. Trench has received several warnings that if he attempts to draw the covers the tenant-farmers will assemble and stone the hounds from the scent. But to all our inquiries Mr. Trench only replied that he has hunted the county for thirty years, and he believes Irishmen to be too good sportsmen to interfere with horse or hound at anyone's bidding, even that of the Land Leaguers.

'Anyhow I am going to put it to the test. I shall listen to no warning, either written or verbal,' he says, waving away a respectably-dressed man who, touching his cap, begs to have a word with Mr. Trench. 'I have hunted the county for thirty years. I shall put the hounds in—yes, I would put them in if you told me the cover was poisoned, and if the tenantry like to throw stones at me and my hounds, they can.'

'They'd be very sorry to do it, yer honour, but we have agreed among ourselves that unless certain——'

The rest of the speech is lost in the pattering of the horses' hoofs. Opening a gate with the end of his riding-whip, Mr. Trench lets himself through, and followed by his hounds and whips, who lash out at the stragglers and call to them to join the pack, he trots across a field towards a large fir-wood. We are all very nervous, our hands twitch at the bridles, and our lips grow dry, for we know not but that the peasants may come out armed with rifles and shoot at us and the hounds; or perhaps they will choose scythes to attack us; and involuntarily we consider the respective advantages of the weapons. Rifle bullets would follow quicker than our horses' heels could take us away, but there is something revolting in the idea of being hacked about by a scythe. There are only about thirty out, and we beg of the ladies to keep back. Quite unmoved, however, Mr. Trench continues to draw the cover. 'Now then, there,' he shouts, 'hunt him out, hunt him out; get to cover, will you! Admiral, get to him, get to him! Ah, hark to Beauty, will you, hark to Beauty! They have got him! Get to him there! Hunt him out! hark to—hark to him there, I say, hark to— Now then, gentlemen, don't ride round the cover, stop in one spot, I beg of you; you are driving him back; tell that fellow there to come back; if he is headed again he'll be chopped, the hounds are close on him!'

At this moment the red varmint is seen stealing across the field, and Beauty and the hounds are getting through the hedge, giving tongue. Mr. Trench blows his horn: 'Gone away, gone away, away again, again.' The blare of the horn rings out over the grey sleepy fields—'gone away.' 'Now then, gentlemen, I beg of you wait until the hounds are out of the cover.'

We have forgotten all the Land Leaguers, and, tense with excitement, we watch the hounds crowding through the fence. Every horse is prancing. A moment more and we shall be riding at that stiff piece of wall, four feet and a half—even now Mr. Manly is advising his wife not to risk the life of the unborn by attempting it. But peasants are climbing that wall: hands, heads, and shoulders appear: they are standing on the top, and are throwing stones at the hounds. Bellringer has been struck, and has run whining from the scent, then half-a-dozen more have stopped short, surprised at the strange interruption.

'Oh, the brutes!' exclaimed Mr. Trench, as he watched a tall thin peasant, a young man dressed in a torn frieze coat, with large pieces of the flannel lining hanging out of the rents, who with a stick is beating the hounds away as they attempt to cross the wall. Others armed with pitchforks and scythes declare that they'll scatter our brains on the grass if we venture to ride over their lands. The stone-throwing is kept up, and a sharp piece of limestone has just struck Sally's horse, and the frightened animal rears violently. This is too much for Molloy, and, regardless of consequences, he touches his horse with the spur and makes for the aggressor. The coward runs like a sheep, and he howls for mercy when the heavy thong of the hunting-whip circles round his shoulders.

'Come on this way, Trench,' cries Molloy, 'we can cross here, and we'll push up the scent farther on.'

'No, no, I have had enough of it; I have seen Irishmen stone my hounds. Well, I thought there was more sport in Irishmen than that; I believe in the country no more.' And blowing his horn the old huntsman collects his hounds round him . . . his last illusions are shattered, the bitterest blow has fallen—Irishmen are no longer sportsmen. After that come what will; he has seen the new era in, he wants to see no more. It is time he should be gathered to his fathers. He will not speak; the affront has sunk into his heart like a dagger . . .

we ask him to come with us, we laugh, we pooh-pooh the whole thing, and declare we shall have better hunting than ever next year, but he shakes his head sorrowfully. And as we go to Mrs. Jack's to lunch, we turn in our saddles and we see the old man riding away, his hounds about him, like one on whom a great calamity has fallen.

'And now, Fleming, mind you, no humbug! I and Sally separately and together will engage Mrs. Jack's attention, at least as much of her attention as it is possible to engage, and you make love to the niece. Try to get her to sit down with you in a corner; anyhow, make the flirtation conspicuous, and we'll have Mrs. Jack nearly mad with rage . . . She is half a savage, you know, and we shall be all probably turned out of the house.'

'But perhaps the girl won't flirt; she may be too shy?'

'Never mind, try to draw her out. Poor little thing, hers is a sad fate! Gee up, old horse! Those brutes of Land Leaguers, Gladstone and Parnell, ought to be hanged.'

CONCLUSION.

The scenes in the pages of this book point to no moral—at least to no moral that I am conscious of; they were not selected to plead any cause, or to announce the success or failure of Land Leaguers or landlords; they were chosen because they seemed to me typical and picturesque aspects of a primitive country and barbarous people. Unconcerned with this or that interest, indifferent to this or that opinion, my desire was to produce a series of pictures to touch the fancy of the reader as a Japanese ivory or fan, combinations of hue and colour calculated to awake in him fictitious feelings of pity, pitiful curiosity and nostalgia of the unknown.

Ireland is a bog, and the aborigines (the Fins) are a degenerate race—short, squat little men—with low foreheads and wide jaws. But the bog, its heather and desolation, and the Fins and their hovels and dirt are as good a subject for brush or pen as an English village clustered round a green—red roofs showing against the foliage of the elms, rows of great sunflowers flaring in the gardens, and quaint windows overgrown with roses.[227] Picturesque comfort or picturesque misery *l'un vaut l'autre*[228] in art, and I sought the picturesque independent of landlords and Land Leaguers; whether one picture is cognate in political feeling with the one that preceded I care not a jot; indeed I would wish each to be evocative of dissimilar impressions, and the whole to produce the blurred and uncertain effect of nature herself.[229] Where the facts seemed to contradict, I let them contradict. Nevertheless, it does not strike me as wholly foreign to, and incompatible with, my method to look upon that which the world terms the serious side of things. The serious side of things I take to mean: first, the direct pecuniary loss or gain; secondly, the indirect, or in other words, the moral loss or gain. I will consider what has been the moral loss or gain to Ireland since she became, under the Parnell *régime*, a free country. Murder, in the first place, is now recognised as a fine art, a popular pastime, and an important factor in politics. Murder? No—boycotting and moonlighting, these are the Parnellite equivalents. 'Murder is unnecessary,' cry the patriots. 'More boycotting, more moonlighting.' And at their bidding, bands of dreamy youths wander about the country at night, breaking into the different cottages, pulling the occupants out of their beds, and shooting in the legs all whom they suspect of wishing to pay their rents, shooting through the head all who might betray them. 'Moonlighting,' Mr. Parnell says, 'is our only preventive against eviction.'[230]

Secondly, the tenants are told that they must pay only a fair rent; and a fair rent is defined as the sum that remains when they have taken what they consider will keep them and their families in decency and comfort. Imagine trying to collect rents anywhere—even in the Champs-Elysées, Parisian, Jovian, or Christian[231]—on such a principle. In 1881 the Irish rents were fixed by law, a fourth was generally struck off, and then the tenant was considered to be assessed at a fair rent.[232] The Coercion Act was then in force, Ireland was profoundly quiet, and the leaders waited. They had not to wait long; party politics rendered its revival impossible, and when the sword was raised outrages began on man and beast. Then in despair, but continuing his dream of settling the Irish question, Gladstone began to consider the probability of Home Rule. Parnell ordered the outrages to cease, and they ceased. But Gladstone failed to carry his Bill. The country was appealed to, and the country by an immense majority decreed against Home Rule. What was to be done? Decidedly moonlighting must begin again. Parnell must feed and clothe his impecunious army.[233] Each ragamuffin costs him two hundred and fifty a year—seventeen thousand five hundred a year—and the pot-boys and nursemaids will want something for their money. Something must be done. No better plan than to bring in a Bill to still further reduce the rents.[234] Say that the judicial rents are not fair rents, that's the idea. Open up the whole question—Gladstone is on his last legs and will vote for anything. The Bill will be thrown out, of course, but it will consolidate us with what remains of the Liberal party and will be a brilliant start for a campaign against rent in Ireland—a campaign against rent, that is to say plenty of moonlighting and boycotting.

Murder and repudiation of debt, such is the doctrine of the League, and insidiously in veiled phrases, in euphemisms of all sorts, the doctrine is preached at land meetings and brooded over, as we have seen, by the cottage fireside. Imagine the ferment produced by these teachings in the minds of a primitive people—and worse than primitive, a people in a retrograde state. Imagine the disintegration of all simple associations of belief, the discarding of all familiar ideas and usages; it is as if all the fibre and nerve of a body were destroyed, pus oozes, and the gases of decay are exhaled, and all the phenomena of dissolution begin—such was Ireland in 1882. Murder had begotten murder, agrarian with political assassination had bred like snakes in dark places, the landlords were forgotten in private animosity, individual hatreds, family misunderstandings had bred in and out and back again to the original stock with riotous longing and brutal lust of cruelty. In 1882 Irish society was coming to pieces like a rotten sponge; the Phoenix Park murders brought the disease to a head;[235] and the Crimes Act came as a saving and a blessing to the poorer tenants who lived in terror of their lives.[236] Tortured and intimidated by the moonlighters, it fell like manna in the desert of their afflictions. Here is one instance which, like one pustule brought under the microscope, reveals the depth of the disease. There are two sisters who do not get on very well together. In the words of the survivor, 'they found it difficult to live in the same house.' One morning, after a quarrel with her sister, Bridget goes out into the potato-field, where a man is digging. She asks him if he can do nothing for her; he scratches his head reflectively and says that he is going to see someone that night, and will speak to him on the subject. On the following day Bridget again goes to meet her friend in the potato-field—of whom, mark you, she knows little or nothing.

He says he talked the matter over last night and it can be done for a pound. But Bridget cannot make up so much money and a bargain is struck, and she pays fifteen shillings to have her sister murdered. A night is chosen, Bridget asks if she may absent herself, she does not care to be in the house on the night her sister is to be murdered; but the man says it might arouse suspicion, and Bridget's scruples are overruled. The murder itself is executed in the latest and most approved fashion. One man mounts on guard, the other enters the hovel at midnight, revolver in hand and shoots the woman dead.[237]

This murder took place at Mullingar, but a jury courageous enough to convict the murderers was not forthcoming, and they escaped. At the time I am speaking of murders and mutilations of man and beast were of daily and nightly occurrence, and I could easily select one for physical barbarity infinitely more repellent, namely, the Maamtrasna murders, which for sullen debauchery and low liquorish cruelty stand unrivalled and unapproached even in the great charnel-house of Irish crime;[238] but the simple Mullingar tragedy, so simple and so free of all melodramatic interest, seems to me more than anything else illustrative of the decay and final dissolution of the moral nature even in its most elementary and original forms.

The priests at first attempted to stem the tide of outrage and murder, but when religion found it was imperilling its own existence it strove to compromise with murder on the Land League platform as it does with the Darwinian theory in the laboratory.

And now to money matters. Let us see if the tenant has benefited pecuniarily by his devotion to Parnell, and to what extent. The Land Act of 1881, by reducing the Irish rents by one fourth or one fifth, puts something like three millions annually into the pockets of the tenants. This is no doubt a very substantial gain, but it is not all gain. First, the lawyers' fees and the cost of the Land Commission ran into a great deal of money; then there were subscriptions—forty thousand pounds had to be collected to pay Parnell for the services he had rendered the Irish tenantry;[239] then there is a continual subscription to the Land League, the ordinary subscription and supplementary subscriptions; subscriptions for the support of the Irish members; subscriptions for the support of evicted tenants, etc. The addition of this is no doubt a good round sum, but it is far from three millions sterling: where does the balance go to? In idleness and drink. Attendance at Land League meetings and political conversations prolonged into the small hours of the morning are not conducive to industry: the land is therefore more neglected than ever, and the tenant is so much more out of pocket.

Since he has become part-proprietor of his holding he has borrowed money at the bank. The bills fall due; they are renewed; the interest keeps running on. In the past he was rendered improvident and thriftless by the uncertainty of his tenure, and the certainty that if he made any improvements they would be confiscated—(I remember when they would not thatch their houses for fear of being evicted)[240]—now having passed from servitude through land meetings[241] and murder, plans to murder and mutilate, he is at once afforded facilities for borrowing of all kinds. Is it possible to conceive a state of things more calculated to destroy whatever remnant of morality political agitation may have left to him? His passions are awakened—but for food, for drink, for dress. Never was an Irish peasant known to spend a penny of his newly-acquired fortune in improving his house, in relegating the pig to a stye, in planting a few flowers that would relieve the intolerable bleakness of his cottage. He spends his share of the money in the public-house, his wife and daughters spend theirs on hideous millinery—dreadful hats with ostrich feathers and shapeless mantles, and tea and eggs for breakfast. Dissoluteness, subscriptions to the Land League, and borrowing money at the banks, have in five years reduced the tenantry to the verge of bankruptcy, and headed by Parnell they again come to their landlords and demand large reductions. And this will occur again and again until the landlords are ruined and the tenants become sole proprietors of their holdings. Nor will it then cease; the banks will insist upon payment of their bills, and worse than the banks, there will be the county usurers (a class of men that Balzac has more than once depicted with terrible eloquence),[242] and several generations will pass before the Irish peasant will be able to hold his own against these men and the temptations they will hold out to him; and were an Irish Parliament sitting in Dublin, unless, indeed property were abolished and a Commune established, I am convinced that in five years' time there would be more evictions carried out by order of the banker and the usurer than there are by the landlords to-day. The Irish peasant has been left a little behind in the march of civilisation: he will have to first conquer the landlords, then he will find himself outdone by banks, usurers, and centuries of inherited idleness and filth, supplemented by ten years of the most infamous moral teaching possible to conceive.[243] When he has overcome these dangers and difficulties he may then be able to take his place as an equal by the side of his Saxon neighbour.

But this is looking very far ahead: let us confine ourselves to considering the issues of to-day's combat. The Parnellite party consists of eighty-five members vowed to render all government in Ireland a farce, and all legislation in England impossible, until England has surrendered autonomy to the Irish people.[244] Eighty-five votes are a terrible weight to be able to throw into either scale; it has already overthrown three Ministers,[245] and with our system of party government, it is impossible to anticipate how many more may not fall before it: and to come to terms with it seems out of the ken of all possibilities: England has been asked the question, and has decided to maintain the Union at all hazards. The fight will then be a terrible unintermittingness of effort. Of Parnell's leadership, it is unnecessary to say a word—the world knows of it; of the ability and courage of some dozen or twenty men grouped around him, I can speak with confidence—some of them are friends of mine, others I know of through their writings. The rest of the party is composed of Mr. Dalys, music-hall managers, and publicans from Liverpool and

Manchester. This tagrag and bobtail is supported principally by subscriptions collected from the nursemaids and pot-boys of New York and Chicago; the immediate object of Mr. Daly is therefore to prove his patriotism by vehemently abusing the landlords, and condoning murder and outrage as ingeniously as his knowledge of the English language allows him. Abuse is his bread, and sophistry is his butter.

This is certainly not very great or very noble, and yet the destiny of the British Empire hangs upon it. For the whole question resolves itself into this:—Will the American nursemaids and potboys continue to subscribe from fifteen to twenty thousand a year to keep Mr. Daly in a cheap lodging, and a cheap dinner, for—let us say[246] a period of ten years? For it is not too much to suppose that, after ten years of obstruction, England would be ready to concede anything? Or, on the other hand, will England return Lord Randolph Churchill to the head of affairs with sufficient majorities to outvote all possible combination that may be brought against him?[247] In ancient times the Goths and Visigoths held the destinies of the Romans, but it is the nursemaids who hold the destinies of the British Empire. A text to ponder on, but I will not ponder . . . I will ask what measures Lord Salisbury[248] and Lord Randolph Churchill adopt to rid themselves of this terrible Irish incubus? In the hopes that the peasant will become Conservative when he is sole owner of his holding, efforts will be made in the direction of peasant proprietary . . . And will the solution of the problem be found in this?

It would be well in accordance with my philosophy, with that view of life which is constitutional to me, to deny the existence of a race-hatred. It would be comforting to hug the belief that if the peasants were owners of the soil they till, that if the exasperatory yearly tributes they are called upon to pay were abolished, that patriotism would exist no longer and that the Celt and the Saxon would henceforth live together in brotherly peace and love. My special temperament inclines me to this view of the question, but when I look Ireland in the face, the face I have known since I was a little child, I find myself obliged to admit the existence of a race-hatred—a hatred as intense and as fierce as that which closes the ferret's teeth on the rat's throat. The Saxon heart is a noble heart, a heart that is ever moved by generous aspirations, a heart that is full of a love of truth and justice. It was these qualities that gave the Saxon the greatest empire the world has ever known, and it will be these very qualities that will now shatter and destroy that empire. The English heart of to-day throbs with an hysterical, with a theoretic, love of justice. For a moment under the pressure of excitement we don the fierce bear-baiting, prize-fighting nature that was once ours; but we have sloughed that nature like a snake its skin, and we can wear it no longer; soon, very soon, we must return to our second self, that self which is now our real self—that self which is now incarnate in Mr. Gladstone and Mr. John Morley.[249] In two years, certainly before the former is eighty, this will be accomplished, and amid praise and acclamation a free Parliament will be given to Ireland. Then the Irish-Americans, those who have subscribed millions of dollars to achieve this, will flock to Ireland, and in seven years all the traces of seven hundred years of Saxon conquest will be effaced. And, looking still farther into the future, I see the inevitable war with Russia beginning on the Afghan frontier,[250] and following on England's first defeat, be the defeat great or small, the Irish Americans who will then be governing in Dublin will declare the independence of their island.

NOTES

NOTES TO INTRODUCTION

1 'Lettres sur l'Irlande' were published on 31 July, 7, 14, 21, 28 August and 4 September 1886.

2 *Terre d'Irlande* par George Moore, transl. M.F. Rabbé (G. Charpentier & Cie., 1887). It was originally to be called *Irlande en Eau Fort* but this was changed at the last moment to *Terre d'Irlande*. Joseph Hone, *The Life of George Moore* (London: Gollancz, 1936), p. 129.

3 Wigram specialised in publishing High Church books of devotion. See Adrian Frazier, *George Moore, 1852-1933* (London and New Haven CT: Yale University Press, 2000), p. 154. He may have been related to to G. V. Wigram (1805-79), a Biblical scholar and uncle by marriage of Charles Stewart Parnell. See R. F. Foster, *Charles Stewart Parnell: The Man and his Family* (Sussex, 1979), pp. 40, 56, 83.

4 In *Terre d'Irlande* the essay entitled 'An Eviction' came before 'A Castle of Yesterday'. A second edition of *Parnell and His Island* was published in 1891, possibly to take advantage of Parnell's death. Edwin Gilcher, 'Collecting Moore', in Janet Egleson Duneavy (ed.), *George Moore in Perspective* (Naas: Malton Press, Gerrards Cross: Colin Smythe, New Jersey: Barnes & Noble, 1983), p. 141. Albert J. Solomon has suggested that the source for the English language title was a book by a minor French writer, Paul Blouet, entitled *John Bull and his Island* (1884). The book was a satirical tour through Britain taken by Max O'Rell (Blouet's pseudonym). Albert J. Solomon, '*Parnell and His Island*: A source for the title', *Notes and Queries* (London) 20 (July 1973): 52-3. It was also to be the source of the title of George Bernard Shaw's play, *John Bull's Other Island* (1904).

5 W. E. Vaughan, *Landlords and Tenants in Ireland, 1848-1904* (Dundalk: Dundalgan Press, 1984), p. 38. The number of net evictions—that is, those evicted minus the number of tenants reinstated as caretakers—rose steadily from 1,900 in 1877; 3,916 in 1878; 5,576 in 1879; 9,436 in 1880; 16,256 in 1881; and 26,003 in 1882. T. W. Moody, *Davitt and Irish Revolution, 1846-82* (Oxford: Clarendon, 1981), pp. 262-3, appendix D1.

6 Of these, there were ten homicides in 1879, eight in 1880 and 22 in 1881. Moody, *Davitt*, p. 565, Appendix E1.

7 Ibid., p. 417.

8 Moore, *Terre d'Irlande*, p. iii.

9 Moore, *Confessions of a Young Man* (London: Swan Sonnenschein, Lowry, 1888), p. 116.

10 Malcolm Brown, *George Moore: A Reconsideration* (Seattle: University of Washington Press, 1955), p. 15.

11 The novels were: *A Modern Lover* (1883); *A Mummer's Wife* (1885); *A Drama in Muslin* (1886); and *A Mere Accident*. The pamphlet was *Literature at Nurse* (1885) an attack on literary censorship by the lending libraries.

12 Moore, *Confessions of a Young Man*, p. 155.

13 Sonja Nejdefors-Frisk, *George Moore's Naturalistic Prose* (Upsala Irish Studies no 3: Upsala, Copenhagen. Dublin and Cambridge, Mass., 1952).

14 Susan L. Mitchell, *George Moore* (Dublin and London: Maunsel, 1916), p. 39.

15 Brendan Fleming, 'French spectacles in an Irish case: from 'Lettres sur l'Irlande' to *Parnell and His Island*', in Alan A. Gillis and Aaron Kelly (eds), *Critical Ireland: New Essays in Literature and Culture* (Dublin: Four Courts, 2001), pp. 69–76.

16 Norman Jeffares, *Anglo-Irish Literature* (Dublin: Gill & Macmillan, 1982), p. 206.

17 NLI 4476/30 Moore to Mrs Moore, undated. Adrian Frazier has dated it to February 1886 (*George Moore*, p. 136).

18 *Freeman's Journal*, 14 August 1880 and *Mayo Examiner*, 4 September 1880; quoted Frazier, *George Moore*, pp. 71–2.

19 Frazier, *George Moore*, p. 84

20 *A Drama in Muslin*, p. 324.

21 Moore was friendly with Eleanor Marx, who introduced him to Ibsen's *A Doll's House* and through whom he may have become acquainted with socialist ideas.

22 Conditions in Dublin in the late nineteenth century are explored in Mary E. Daly, *Dublin: The Deposed Capital: A Social and Economic History, 1860–1914* (Cork: Cork University Press, 1984).

23 Similar ambivalent attitudes to Castle society on the part of Moore's contemporary, the artist Rose Barton, are discussed in Vera Kreilkamp, '*Going to the Levée* as Ascendancy spectacle: Alternative narratives in an Irish painting', in Adele M. Dalsimer (ed.), *Visualizing Ireland: National Identity and the Pictorial Tradition* (London: Faber & Faber, 1993), pp. 37–54. I am grateful to Margaret Kelleher for bringing this study to my attention.

24 Decades later, Lady Fingall found Moore's name in the Dublin Castle Dinner Book and Drawing Room Book: 'There was, surprisingly, Mr George Moore, Moore Hall, County Mayo, staying at the Shelbourne Hotel, a young man up from the bogs and lakes of Mayo for the Dublin Season.' *Seventy Years Young: Memories of Elizabeth, Countess of Fingall* (2nd edn, Dublin: Lilliput, 1991). Her husband, Lord Fingall, the State Steward,

was one of the Castle officials that Moore had lampooned, while the Chamberlain, Colonel Dease, with whom Moore had corresponded, was Fingall's cousin.

25 *Freeman's Journal*, 9 February 1885, p. 4. The paper sprang to Moore's defence, pointing out that 'the social favour of the Castle, even to those who brave attendance at the Levée, is as much a matter of patronage, favour, flunkeyism, and dodge as its political rewards. Mr George Moore is a gentleman of high social position, son of the late George Henry Moore, landed proprietor and Member of Parliament. Mr George Moore is himself High Sheriff nominate, and next on the list for the Shrievalty of Mayo. But he is also a man of letters, and such are not very acceptable to Castle folk.'

26 NLI MS 2648/2/10, McCarthy to GM, 18 February 1885.

27 In *A Drama in Muslin*, May Gould remarks to her friend Alice: 'Just fancy going to all this expense to be kissed by the Lord-Lieutenant: a man one never saw before,' and asks: 'Will you be ashamed when he kisses you?' (p. 168).

28 Among these are: *A Mummer's Wife* (1885), *A Drama in Muslin* (1886), *Esther Waters* (1894).

29 The Barton girls and their mother stayed there in *A Drama in Muslin*.

30 *Memories of the Countess of Fingall*, p. 60.

31 In fact, Moore was a benevolent landlord, as his father, George Henry Moore, had been, and he was in no danger of assassination by his tenants. Brown, *George Moore: A Reconsideration*, pp. 17–18.

32 NLI MS 4479/26, George Moore to Mary Blake Moore, October 1886.

33 Frazier, *George Moore*, p. 141.

34 In *Ave*, vol. 1 of *Hail and Farewell* (London: Heinemann, 1911) he writes how in his childhood he was given to understand that he was 'such an ugly little boy that nobody else [apart from a beggar woman] would marry me . . . I could see that he [his father] thought me a stupid little boy, and was ashamed of me . . .' (p. 81). In *Salve*, vol. 2 of *Hail and Farewell* (London: Heinemann, 1912), p. 106, he reminisced about being taunted as a child by the Blakes when he claimed to have met the King of the Fairies on the rocks at the end of Kingstown (now Dun Laoghaire) pier.

35 Elizabeth Grubgeld, *George Moore and the Autogenous Self: The Autobiography and Fiction* (Syracuse: Syracuse University Press, 1994) p. 33.

36 *A Drama in Muslin*, pp. 123–5.

37 Deborah Fleming, '*A Man Who Does not Exist*': The Irish Peasant in the Work of W. B. Yeats and J. M. Synge* (Ann Arbor: University of Michigan Press, 1995), p. 51.

38 *Confessions of a Young Man*, p. 99.

39 Ibid., p. 26.

40 For example, Father Brosnan in Anthony Trollope's, *The Landleaguers* (1882); or Father Frank in Letitia McClintock's *A Boycotted Household* (1881).

41 For example, Father Daly in Rosa Mulholland's *Marcella Grace* (1886) or Father Phil O'Sullivan in William O'Brien's *When We Were Boys* (1890).

42 Like the priest in *A Drama in Muslin*, this character is probably based on the parish priest of Ardrahan, Fr Thomas B. Considine. Edward Martyn's mother was so outraged by his depiction in *A Drama in Muslin* that she told her son that her nephew, Moore, must never again enter Tillyra Castle while she lived. (Hone, *Life of George Moore*, p. 124).

43 *Terre d'Irlande*, pp. 161–2.

44 Donald Jordan, *Land and Popular Politics in Ireland: County Mayo from the Plantation to the Land War* (Cambridge: Cambridge University Press, 1994), p. 267.

45 Grubgeld, *George Moore*, pp. 30–1. Moody, *Davitt*, pp. 391–5.

46 Gerard Moran, 'James Daly and the rise and fall of the Land League in the west of Ireland, 1879–82,' *Irish Historical Studies* XXIX 114 (November 1994): 189–207; Donald Jordan, 'John O'Connor Power, Charles Stewart Parnell and the centralisation of popular politics in Ireland', *Irish Historical Studies* XXV, 97 (May 1986): 46–66.

47 T. M. Healy, *Letters and Leaders of My Day* (2 vols, London, 1928), I, p. 65. Power is believed to have been the illegitimate son of a policeman and spent some of his childhood in Ballinasloe workhouse.

48 Jordan claims that during the years 1874–84, he was 'the most enigmatic, controversial and divisive figure in Irish politics'. 'John O'Connor Power', p. 46. It was Power who had first persuaded Moore's father to stand for parliament in 1868–9. Ibid., p. 48.

49 Frazier, *George Moore*, p. 73.

50 Brendan Fleming, 'French Spectacles in an Irish Case: From 'Letters sur l'Irlande to *Parnell and His Island*', Alan A. Gillis and Aaron Kelly (eds), *Critical Ireland: New Essays in Literature and Culture* (Dublin: Four Courts, 2001), p. 74.

51 In Moore's last autobiographical work, *A Communication to My Friends*, written in 1933, he again praised Lord Ardilaun. See Hone, *Life of George Moore*, p. 129.

52 However, Ardilaun, despite his philanthropy, was never part of Plunkett's movement and there was a long dispute between the two men over the role of the Royal Dublin Society. Trevor West, *Horace Plunkett: Co-operation and Politics, an Irish Biography* (Gerrards Cross: Colin Smythe and Washington: Catholic University of America Press, 1986), pp. 49–51; Carla King, 'Horace Plunkett: defender of the Union', in

George Boyce and Alan O'Day (eds), *Defenders of the Union: A Survey of British and Irish Unionism since 1801* (London and New York: Routledge, 2001), pp. 137–58.

53 Carla King, 'Some late Victorian novels and the Irish land question', in Neil McCaw (ed.), *Writing Irishness in Nineteenth-Century British Culture* (Aldershot: Ashgate, forthcoming, 2004).

54 *A Drama in Muslin*, pp. 322–4.

55 Quoted in G. Jean-Aubry, 'George Moore and Emile Zola', *The Bookman's Journal* XI, 39 (1924): 98–100. In his turn, Moore considered *La Terre* to be Zola's finest novel. Ibid., p. 100.

56 Frazier, *George Moore*, pp. 141, 504 n.122.

57 Anthony Trollope included a depiction of 'stopping the hunt' in his last novel *The Landleaguers* (1883).

58 NLI 4479/19, Moore to his mother, 17 February 1884.

59 *A Drama in Muslin*, p. 193.

60 Laurence M. Geary, *The Plan of Campaign, 1886–91* (Cork: Cork University Press, 1986).

61 His charge was unfair as farmers had encountered renewed difficulties. By 1886 agricultural production had fallen to 79 per cent of its 1881 level and compared with the average for the four preceding years, the value of livestock and crops fell by 18½ per cent in 1885 and 1886. Poor weather, soil exhaustion and increased foreign competition were held responsible. The falling agricultural prices were accompanied by a general restriction of credit on the part of banks, shops and moneylenders. Geary, *The Plan of Campaign*, p. 6.

62 The book was given its English title after the articles were written and it may be that Parnell's name was used to attract a wider market. On the other hand, this does not explain Moore's avoidance of any detailed discussion of the dominant Irish figure of his day. This offers an intriguing parallel with the attitude of Oscar Wilde, examined in W. J. Mc Cormack, 'Wilde and Parnell' in Jerusha McCormack (ed.), *Wilde the Irishman* (New Haven CT: Yale University Press, 1998), pp. 95–102.

63 Grubgeld, *George Moore*, p. 21.

64 Ibid., p. 2. Patrick Ward suggests that 'Moore with his aptitude for excess became a triple "exile", alienated from Ireland, France and England, displaying and living out all the characteristics of [Edward] Said's intellectual exile . He was restless, unsettled, one who succeeded in unsettling others and one who could not return "home". He was an artist for whom writing became a place to live.' 'Exile, Art and Alienation: George Moore's Irish Writings', in Patrick Ward, *Exile, Emigration and Irish Writing* (Dublin, Irish Academic Press, 2002), p. 231.

65 Frazier, *George Moore*, p. xiv.

66 Moore, *Confessions of a Young Man*, p. 99.

67 Mitchell, *George Moore*, p. 59.

68 *Freeman's Journal*, 21 August 1886, p. 4.

69 *Westminster Review*, no. 128 (June 1887), p. 374.

70 *Academy*, vol. 21 (2 April 1887), p. 235.

71 'Paris day by day', *Daily Telegraph*, 14 February 1887.

72 A. [Mary] F. Robinson, 'A Letter from England', *Literary World* (Boston), 11 June 1887, p. 184.

73 John S. Kelly, *The Bodyke Evictions* (Ennis: Fossabeg Press, 1987).

74 Frazier, *George Moore*, p. 154.

75 King, 'Some late Victorian novels'.

76 See for example, James H. Murphy, *Catholic Fiction and Social Reality in Ireland, 1873–1922* (Greenwood, CT: Greenwood Press, 1997) where, as he puts it:

The members of the upper middle class viewed their task as being to modify the adverse image that Ireland had been allotted in English cultural discourse in order not only to increase the esteem in which they were held but to increase their own self-esteem. In some respects it was a classical, colonial problem: an assimilationist class balking at the fact that its country was still being considered 'native' (p. 17).

Elsewhere, Murphy suggests that 'Moore can be seen as a counter to the work of the *Irish Monthly* group', a circle of social Catholic writers. James H. Murphy, *Ireland: A Social, Cultural and Literary History, 1791–1891* (Dublin: Four Courts, 2003), p. 164.

77 Hone, *Life of George Moore*, p. 224.

78 Moore, *Salve*, p. 11.

79 Mitchell, *George Moore*, p. 68.

80 Moore, Preface to 1921 edition of *The Lake;* quoted by Edwin Gilcher, 'Collecting Moore', in Janet Egleson Dunleavy, *George Moore in Perspective* (Naas: Malton Press; Gerrard's Cross: Colin Smythe; New Jersey: Barnes & Noble, 1983), p. 134. Here he was using the analogy of a Renaissance school of painters, in which the individual artist is not identifiable but the dominant influence is attributed to a known master.

81 Quoted in Frank Tuohy, *Yeats* (London: Macmillan, 1976), p. 214.

NOTES TO PARNELL AND HIS ISLAND

1   The view described here is from Vico Road, looking down over Dublin Bay.

2   Here the metaphor shifts from a comparison with a painting by Turner to one reminiscent of a pre-Raphaelite image.

3   The beach at Killiney.

4 Moore was quite sympathetic to socialist ideas. In 1885 he had an affair with Olive Schreiner, whose ideas on 'the woman question' are believed to have influenced Moore's novel, *A Drama in Muslin: A Realistic Novel* (London: Vixatelly, 1886). Schreiner moved in socialist circles and introduced Moore to Eleanor Marx, on whom he based the heroine of his play, *The Strike at Arlingford* (London: Walter Schott, 1893). See Adrian Frazier, *George Moore 1852–1933* (London and New Haven CT: Yale University Press, 2000), pp. 126–7.

5 It is unclear why Moore puts this passage into inverted commas. He is evidently expressing his own dilemma.

6 He is referring to the land war, which began in 1879.

7 Rent was paid twice yearly, on gale days, generally in May and November.

8 Vous n'y trouverez pas non plus d'escaliers montant d'une rue à une autre comme à Paris. Dublin a l'air d'une aquarelle dessinée par une vieille gouvernante. (*Terre*, p. 15) [Neither does one find there steps linking one street with another, as in Paris. Dublin has the appearance of an aquarelle drawn by an old governess.]

9 . . . des cours exhalant l'odeur nauséabonde des fosses aux ordures non vidées (*Terre*, p. 15). [the yards give off the sickening smell of unemptied rubbish pits.]

10 Lord Ardilaun.

11 Il continue à donner à la ville cette apparence de friperie qui caractérise si bien Dublin. (*Terre*, p. 18) [It continues to lend to the city that appearance of a second-hand clothes dealer so characteristic of Dublin.]

12 In *A Drama in Muslin*, it is depicted as: 'melancholy Merrion Square! broken pavements, unpainted hall-doors, rusty area railings, meagre outside curs hidden almost out of sight in the deep gutters—how infinitely pitiful' (p. 158). Moore's mother, Mary Blake Moore had taken a house in Merrion Square for the Horse Show in August 1880 and he stayed there at that time.

13 Dublin Castle, the centre of British government in Ireland, discussed in the next section of this chapter.

14 William Makepeace Thackeray's novel *Vanity Fair: A Novel Without a Hero* was first published in volume form in 1848.

15 In *Terre d'Irlande* (p. 19), what follows is shortened to: 'j'ai rencontré un *clubman* qui me crut, lorsque je lui dis que Richard Wagner était un grand éleveur de bêtes à cornes.' [I met a clubman who believed me when I told him that Richard Wagner was a great livestock breeder.]

16 The Kildare Street Club, discussed on p. 12.

17 Moore was a fan of Wagner's music, which is a theme in his novel *Evelyn Innes* (London: T. Fisher Unwin, 1898). He attended the Wagner

Festival at Bayreuth five times. His trip in 1899 with Edward Martyn is
described in *Ave*, the first volume of Moore's memoir, *Hail and Farewell*
(London: Heinemann, 1911).

18 Un étranger pourrait le prendre pour un magasin à poudre. (*Terre*,
p. 22) [A foreigner could mistake it for a powder magazine.]

19 C'est une de ces rues que les officiers du château choisirent pour y
perpétrer des crimes inconnus jusqu'ici dans les fastes de la honte, crimes
dévoilés à la lumière par l'énergie de M. O'Brien, un Parnelliste membre
du Parlement; crimes dont les empereurs romains déguisaient l'horreur
en les environnant de marbre, de soie et d'or, mais dont l'abomination
est centuplée ici par l'entourage, la saleté et les ordures de Ship Street.
Quelquefois, comme chez le vieux Cenci de Shelley, la conscience de son
péché, son insouciante résolution de défier Dieu peut élever le coupable
à une certaine terreur tragique; mais le défaut de perception morale, au
lieu de diminuer l'horreur et le dégoût d'une luxure contre nature, semble
l'accroître au contraire; et de tout ce que le hasard ou une indiscrète
curiosité a pu déterrer dans l'égout du péché, je ne connais rien de plus
terrible que l'histoire de l'homme aveugle, le gardien de la maison,
l'histoire de ces boucs, de ces vieux libertins de soixante ans qui lisaient
en tête-à-tête la Bible aux soldats. L'archevêque fut obligé de lancer un
mandement pastoral défendant à ses ouailles de lire les journaux pendant les débats du procès. (*Terre*, pp. 23–4) [It is one of those streets that
the Castle officers chose for the perpetration of crimes unheard of until
now in the realms of disgrace, crimes brought to light by the efforts of
Mr O'Brien, Parnellite member of Parliament. The Roman emperors
disguised the horror of such crimes by surrounding them with marble,
silk and gold, but their abomination is multiplied by a hundredfold by the
surroundings, the dirt and filth of Ship Street. Sometimes, as in the case
of Shelley's old Censi, the awareness of his sin, or his naïve intention to
defy God may rouse in the guilty person a certain tragic terror; but the
lack of moral perception, rather than reducing the horror and disgust of
an unnatural lust, seems rather to increase it; and for all that fate or an
indiscrete curiosity could unearth in the sewer of sin, I never knew
anything more terrible than the story of the blind man who was the
caretaker of the house; the story of these goats, these old libertines of
sixty who used to read the Bible in private to the soldiers. The archbishop was obliged to issue a pastoral decree forbidding his flock from
reading the papers during the debates on the proceedings.] Moore is here
referring to a scandal that arose following the publication on 25 August
1883 of an article in *United Ireland*, in which T. M. Healy accused James
Ellis French, Detective Director in the Royal Irish Constabulary, of sex-
ually harassing some younger police officers. Following further allegations

in the newspaper, trials were held in August 1884 of eight men on charges of homosexual practices. Four were found guilty and sentenced to penal servitude.

20 Also referred to as the Lord Lieutenant, the Viceroy was the British monarch's representative in Ireland, and resided at the Viceregal Lodge in Phoenix Park, Dublin.

21 Until 1958 young British debutantes were presented to the reigning monarch in a formal ceremony.

22 This scene is satirised in *A Drama in Muslin*: 'And now a lingering survival of the terrible Droit de Seigneur—diminished and attenuated, but still circulating though our modern years—this ceremony, a pale ghost of its former self, is performed; and, having received a kiss on either cheek, the *débutantes* are free to seek their bridal beds in Patrick's Hall' (p. 175).

23 'about a putrefying carcass' omitted in *Terre d'Irlande*.
. . . autour d'un excrément de choix! (*Terre*, p. 27) [around a choice excrement].

24 Aides de camp.

25 In 1887 there were thirty officers in the Lord Lieutenant's household alone. *Thom's Directory* (Dublin: Thom & Co., 1887), p. 785.

26 Une femme faisant le sacrifice de sa vertu pour sauver la vie de son mari a toujours été pour les dramaturges une situation favorite; je ne dis pas que si un romancier, mettant en scène le Château de Dublin, représentait une mère se soumettant à tous les caprices d'un chambellan en vue d'obtenir une carte pour un des bals privés de la cour, il n'exagérait pas la situation; mais s'il se contentait d'écrire que l'adultère a été souvent payée avec une carte d'invitation, il ne dirait que l'exacte vérité. J'ai souvent jeté les regards vers certain sofa de ce palais, en regrettant que les sofas n'eussent pas de langue. (*Terre*, p. 30) [A woman sacrificing her virtue to save her husband's life has always been a favourite situation for dramatists. I cannot say whether a novelist, setting his scene in Dublin Castle would be exaggerating the situation in representing the mother as succumbing to all the advances of the Chamberlain with a view to obtaining an invitation to one of the private balls at the Castle, but if he confined himself to saying that an adulterer has often been paid with an invitation, he would be speaking no more than the literal truth. I have often glanced at a certain sofa at this palace regretting the fact that sofas cannot speak.]

27 Founded in 1824 and remodelled along more elegant lines in 1866, the Shelbourne Hotel was at this time the main hotel of the Irish Ascendancy. Moore stayed there in 1884, while researching his novel, *A Drama in Muslin*. See James Liddy, 'George Moore's Dublin' in Janet Egleson Dunleavy, *George Moore in Perspective* (Naas: Malton Press;

Gerrard's Cross: Colin Smythe; New Jersey: Barnes & Noble, 1983), pp 58–68; Elizabeth Bowen, *The Shelbourne Hotel* (New York: Knopf, 1951).

28 This is a misspelling of her name [Vauquer—spelled correctly in *Terre d'Irlande*]. Mme Vauquer was a widow who kept a 'bourgeois boarding house' in Balzac's novel, *Père Goriot*.

29 In *Terre d'Irlande* this is given as £3. 10s.

30 Gustave Flaubert (1821–80) famous French novelist, was born and educated at Rouen. He studied law in Paris but thereafter devoted himself to literature. His care for accurate documentation won him a reputation as a master of the *réalistes*, but he was not fundamentally a realistic novelist. His most famous work was *Madame Bovary* (1857). See Paul Harvey and J. E. Heseltine, *The Oxford Companion to French Literature* (Oxford: Clarendon, 1959), pp. 274–5. Moore was particularly influenced by Flaubert's writing as he began to move away from the influence of Zola in the mid-1880s.

31 . . . dit une des vieilles filles (*Terre*, p. 32) [says one of the old maids].

32 In *Terre d'Irlande* this is given as 'mille livres à l'année' [a thousand pounds a year].

33 A Dublin, une vierge a, pour ainsi dire, la virginité du vice; l'adultère et les invitations du Château sont les seuls thèmes de la conversation. La veilleur de nuit est son héros. Elle sait parfaitement comment, une nuit, il ferma la porte de M. X. . . , pendant que celui-ci était dans la chambre de mistress Y. . . , et comment le pauvre homme ne put rentrer dans sa chambre et dut rester cinq heures au *water-closet*; elle sait très bien aussi comment le veilleur avait reçu l'ordre de tenir un compte exact des heures que le capitaine A. . . passait dans le salon de lady B. . . (le salon conduit à la chambre à coucher), et comment, lorsque le compte fut fait, il se trouva que le captaine avait passé en une semaine quarante heures en tête-à-tête avec sa seigneurie. Un titre est un titre; mais quarante heures d'adultère par semaine, c'était par trop fort: Lady B. . . fut priée de décamper, et une médaille de bonne conduite fut décernée au veilleur. (*Terre*, pp. 34–5) [In Dublin a virgin is, so to say, a virgin in vice—adultery and invitations to the Castle are the sole topics of conversation. The night watchman is its hero. She knows perfectly how, one night, he closed Mr X. . .'s door while he was in Mrs Y. . .'s room and how the poor man could not get back into his own room and had to remain in the water closet for five hours; she also knows how the watchman was ordered to keep an exact record of the time that Captain A. . . spent in Lady B . . .'s drawing-room (the drawing-room leads directly to the bedroom), and how, when counted, it turned out the captain had spent forty hours tête-à-tête with her ladyship in one week. A title is a title but forty hours of adultery—that is too much: Lady B. . . was asked to leave, and the watchman was given a medal for good conduct.]

34 The Kildare Street Club was founded in 1782 at 6 Kildare Street. It later built new premises on the corner of Kildare Street and Nassau Street. In the 1880s it had between 600 and 700 members, paying an annual subscription of £10. See R. B. McDowell, *Land and Learning: Two Irish Clubs* (Dublin: Lilliput, 1993).

35 . . . Comme les huîtres aussi, les vieux fossiles regardent à travers leur fenêtre. Cette fenêtre est le Club. . . (*Terre*, p. 36) [like oysters too, the old fossils look through the window. This window is the Club. . .].

36 The Liberal Prime Minister, William Ewart Gladstone (1809–98) had introduced Land Acts in 1870 and 1881, which had the effect of curbing the power of landlords to raise rents and evict tenants. He was also responsible for introducing the First Home Rule Bill in 1886, which the Unionist landlords opposed.

37 Moore is describing a passing demonstration by members of the Irish National League (successor to the Land League).

38 . . . de l'hotel Shelbourne (*Terre*, p. 37) [. . . from the Shelbourne Hotel].

39 Mrs Rusville appears as Mrs Symonds in *A Drama in Muslin*.

40 'sometimes hand in hand laid gently' omitted in *Terre d'Irlande*.
. . . Presque couchées dans les bras l'une de l'autre . . . (*Terre*, p. 38) [. . . almost resting in each other's arms].

41 Cork Hill is the hill on which Dublin Castle was built.

42 This appears to be a reference to the possible passage of Irish Home Rule, although the first Home Rule Bill had been defeated on 6 June 1886. Gladstone was to introduce a second Home Rule Bill, also unsuccessful, in 1893.

43 Moore's cousins, the Ruttledges, believed this to be a description of their home, Cornfield, County Mayo. See NLI 14479/26, Moore to Mary Blake Moore, October 1886.

44 The Land League had been succeeded by the Irish National League in October 1882. Neither organisation ever advocated violence against landlords. However, the land conflict released a good deal of local aggression against landlords and others, for which the Land League and National League were held responsible.

45 Moore is taking his uncle and former agent, Joe Blake, as an example.

46 The *British Sportsman* had a short existence in the 1880s before it merged, around 1892, into *Shooting Times*.

47 This sentence is omitted in *Terre d'Irlande*.

48 Saville Row. In *Terre d'Irlande* this is given as: un habitué des boulevards [one used to the boulevards] (p. 47).

49 Moore is referring to his own family house, Moore Hall, and himself as the absent poet.

50　Partree Mountains.

51　This is the village of Carnacun, just down the hill from Moore Hall, see Frazier, *George Moore*, p. 74.

52　'a stink which the inmates describe as "a warm smell"' omitted in *Terre d'Irlande*.

Les habitants appellent la fermentation de la vase et de la sueur une odeur chaude. (*Terre*, p. 52) [The locals call the fermentation of ooze and sweat a warm smell].

53　Un docteur du pays m'a raconté cette histoire. Il avait été envoyé pour soigner un enfant dont les boyaux sortaient. On avait laissé l'enfant dormant sur le bord du berceau, et la couverture était tombée; le cochon s'approcha et mordit le bout des boyaux, et quand le docteur arriva, il se trouva que l'opération faite par le cochon avait parfaitement réussi. (*Terre*, p. 53) [A local doctor told me this story. He had been sent to attend a child whose intestine protruded. The child had been left sleeping on the side of the cradle and the cover had slipped off; the pig approached and bit the end of the intestine, and when the doctor arrived, he found that the operation performed by the pig was completely successful.]

54　'there is little butter-milk' omitted in *Terre d'Irlande*.

. . . et un peu de lait s'ajoute au repas (*Terre*, p. 54) [and a little milk is added to the meal].

55　'Beautiful sentiments blossom in the soul when fortune begins to gild the furniture.' Honoré de Balzac (1799–1850) was born at Tours of Midi peasant stock. He studied at the Collège des Oratorians at Vendôme and in a private school in Paris. He worked in lawyer's office but from 1819 devoted himself to writing. He produced some 91 novels and tales between 1829 and 1848, as well as a great deal of journalism. See Harvey and Heseltine, *Oxford Companion to French Literature*, p. 46. Moore was greatly influenced by Balzac's writing. He wrote to his mother from Paris: 'I read now nothing but Balzac, Hugo, Shakespeare, the Bible and a couple of new novels every year and a volume or two of verse.' NLI MS 4479/11 Moore to Mary Blake Moore, undated.

56　'Irish Celt' omitted in *Terre d'Irlande*.

. . . d'un paysan irlandais (*Terre*, p. 55) [an Irish peasant].

57　'Driving along the bleak roads' omitted in *Terre d'Irlande*.

Nous avançons en suivant des routes d'une nudité désolante; nous avons des *policemen* devant nous et derrière nous (*Terre*, p. 56) [we advance along bare and desolate roads; we have policemen before and behind us].

58　'This is Lake Mount' omitted in *Terre d'Irlande*.

. . . la maison qui couronne cette large colline verte est le Lake Mount, . . . (*Terre*, pp. 56–7) [the house that crowns this large green hill is Lake Mount]. Moore Hall.

59 The house was built by Moore's great-grandfather, George Moore (1729–99), who had made his fortune in Alicante and its design, including the balcony, was influenced by Spanish house styles.

60 The family motto was: '*Fortis cedere, cedere non potest*' [He who proceeds with courage will never fail]. The date of construction of the house was 1792.

61 'in the sun' omitted in *Terre d'Irlande*.
. . . et le large feuillage des hêtres se balance avec la mélancolique langueur d'un éventail. (*Terre*, p. 58) [. . . and the broad foliage of the beech trees rocks with the melancholy languor of a fan]. This description of the house and its setting is somewhat reminiscent of the first chapter of Balzac's *Les Paysans*, entitled 'Le château'.

62 . . . que personne ne connaît,—arrive à la porte dans une voiture de poste (*Terre*, p. 59) [whom no one knows, arrives at the door in a post carriage].

63 . . . Personne ne le connaît [no one knows him]. This is Moore's description of his younger self.

64 This is Joseph Appleby, the stewart.

65 'Mr.—— lent the house.' is omitted in *Terre d'Irlande*.

66 Il avait toujours eu du goût pour les choses qu'il ne pouvait pas tout à fait comprendre. «Quand, disait-il, on est parvenu à comprendre à fond un opéra, un livre ou un tableau, une grande partie du charme a disparu.» A dix-huit ans, il avait entrepris le tour du monde en quête d'un art qu'il ne pût pas tout à fait comprendre; et comme il avait rencontré beaucoup de choses en ce genre sur le boulevard Montmartre, il y était resté jusqu'à l'âge de trente ans. Le mauvais état de ses affaires l'avait ramené en Irlande. (*Terre*, p. 61) [He had always had a taste for things that he could not quite comprehend. 'When one has come to fully understand an opera, a book or a picture, a large part of the charm is gone,' he said. At eighteen he had undertaken a tour of the world in search of an art that he could not fully comprehend, and as he had found many things of this kind on the boulevard Montmartre, he had remained there until the age of thirty. The bad state of his affairs had called him back to Ireland.]

67 Charles Baudelaire (1821–67) poet and critic—one of the main nineteenth-century influences on modern poetry. He was born in Paris and educated at Lyons and Paris. His most famous work is his collection of poems, *Les Fleurs du mal* (1857); six of the poems were banned and he was prosecuted and fined for offences to public morals. See Harvey and Heseltine, *Oxford Companion to French Literature*, pp. 53–4.

68 Paul Verlaine (1844–96) was born at Metz but educated in Paris, where he worked as a clerk. With Mallarmé and Baudelaire he founded the so-called Decadent movement later became leader of the Symbolist poets. See Harvey and Heseltine, *Oxford Companion to French Literature*, pp. 738–9.

69 'Indeed, he hated . . . rent with them.' omitted in *Terre d'Irlande*.
En tenant compte des modifications d'âge et de tempérament, on rencontre assez fréquemment aujourd'hui ce type d'hommes en Irlande. De tous les coins du monde, ils sont revenus à leur pays natal. (*Terre*, p. 62) [Taking account of differences of age and temperament, one meets this kind of man quite frequently in Ireland. They return to their native land from all countries of the world.]

70 Moore describes the house and gardens as neglected and decrepit here but when it was destroyed by anti-Treaty nationalists in 1923 he wrote: 'The burning of Moore Hall affected me more deeply than anything else could, more than anything I thought could; it has gone to the roots.' John Eglinton, *Letters of George Moore* (Bournemouth: Sydenham & Co, 1942), p. 64.

71 'the room is an exact copy of a Greek chamber' omitted in *Terre d'Irlande*.
. . . c'est une vrai chambre de palais (*Terre*, p. 64) [it's a palatial room].

72 'that would do violence to the taste of a retired soap-boiler' omitted in *Terre d'Irlande*.

73 Like a Keepsake beauty drawn by Westhall.

74 Castle Carra, described in 'A castle of yesterday'.

75 'But to-day as well as yesterday is in ruins.' omitted in *Terre d'Irlande*.

76 Moore's father, George Henry Moore, twice won the Chester cup: once on Coranna in 1846, which brought him £17,000; and again in 1861 his horse called Croaghpatrick won the races at Goodwood and Chester, bringing him just under £20,000.

77 Long dead.

78 *La Vogue* was a well-known Symbolist weekly review. Thirty-two numbers were published from 1836. See Harvey and Heseltine, *Oxford Companion to French Literature*, p. 751.

79 Stéphane Mallarmé (1842–98) was born and studied in Paris. He worked as a schoolmaster and became the centre of a group of French Symbolist poets in the 1880s. See Harvey and Heseltine, *Oxford Companion to French Literature*, pp. 441–2. He was a friend of Edouard Manet and, through him, of George Moore.

80 Old servant: Joseph Applely.

81 Here Moore is probably describing his uncle, Joseph Blake.

82 'vingt' [twenty] in *Terre d'Irlande*, p. 69.

83 This exchange is almost identical to that between Arthur Barton and his tenants in *A Drama in Muslin*, pp. 124–5.

84 'capital year' omitted in *Terre d'Irlande*.
. . . une bien mauvaise année (*Terre*, p. 71) [a very bad year].

85 Maize meal was imported and used to supplement the diet of the poor throughout the second half of the nineteenth century. See E. Margaret Crawford, 'Indian meal and pellagra in nineteenth-century Ireland', in J. M. Goldstrom, and L. A. Clarkson (eds), *Irish Population, Economy, and Society: Essays in Honour of the Late K.H. Connell* (Oxford: Clarendon, 1981), pp. 113–33); and E. Margaret Crawford and L. A. Clarkson, *Feast and Famine: A History of Nutrition in Ireland, 500–1920* (Oxford: Oxford University Press, 2001).

86 'any more than yours will' omitted in *Terre d'Irlande*.
. . . votre bon vouloir (*Terre*, p. 73) [for your goodwill].

87 The tenants are threatening to kill any new landlord.

88 The official valuation of land for tax purposes was carried out between 1853 and 1865 under the direction of Richard Griffith and was often referred to as 'Griffith's valuation'. It was based on the average prices for 1849–51 and was not readjusted in subsequent years to conform to the increased value of agricultural land. The tenant side, while well aware that the valuation did not reflect market prices, used Griffith's valuation as the basis for what they considered a fair rent. See Barbara L. Solow, *The Land Question and the Irish Economy, 1870–1903* (Cambridge, Mass.: Harvard University Press, 1971), pp. 61–8.

89 The outlying estates were at Ashbrook, Bellavary and Gallen, County Mayo.

90 Here Moore is amalgamating two people. His ancestor who was buried at the ruined chapel was John Moore (b. 1706) but the man who built Moore Hall was George Moore of Alicante. See Frazier, *George Moore*, pp. 6, 74–5.

91 'He seemed however determined to meet his fate.' Omitted in *Terre d'Irlande*.

92 What follows is based on a visit Moore made in October 1880.

93 Castlebar.

94 'Two kinds . . . law of life.' Omitted in *Terre d'Irlande*.
Les paysans n'ont qu'à choisir entre les deux (*Terre*, p. 79) [the peasants have only to choose between the two]. This portrait may be based on Father Patrick Lavelle, the Fenian priest of Partree, who gave the funeral oration at George Henry Moore's funeral in 1870. Frazier, *George Moore*, p. 74.

95 'We do not readily understand . . . arid land.' Omitted in *Terre d'Irlande*.

96 This is probably one of Moore's own tenants.

97 James Hack Tuke (1819–96) was an English Quaker banker and philanthropist who first became involved in Ireland when he assisted William Edward Forster in famine relief during the Great Famine. With a recurrence of agricultural crisis, he set up a fund, which became known

as Mr Tuke's Fund, to carry out a comprehensive scheme of family emigration. In all, some 9,500 tenants were assisted in emigration to the United States, with an expenditure of £70,000. Emigration from Mayo was to rise to unprecedented numbers in 1881, most of it unassisted. Jordan, *Land and Popular Politics in Ireland: County Mayo from the Plantation to the Land War* (Cambridge and New York: Cambridge University Press, 1994), p. 282.

98 The tomb of John Moore, father of George Moore of Alicante, Moore's great-great-grandfather.

99 'almost hidden . . . growth of nettles' omitted in *Terre d'Irlande*.

100 George Moore of Alicante.

101 George Henry Moore.

102 George Augustus Moore.

103 D'après la carte, l'Irlande se compose de quatre provinces; j'ai montré dans mon seconde chapitre comment Dublin se divise en quatre parties; je diviserai aujourd'hui la société irlandaise en quatre classes: les propriétaires, les fermiers-tenanciers, les prêtres et les patriotes. Je pourrais sans doute subdiviser encore chacune de ses classes en quatre; mais le pays est si primitif et si barbare que la première division est bien suffisante. Elle est même très complète, et en évitant les extrêmes, en choisissant ce qui me semble de plus typique dans chaque classe, je pourrai indiquer les lignes principales qui constituent la société irlandaise. (*Terre*, pp. 85–6) [According to the map, Ireland is made up of four provinces. I have shown in my second chapter how Dublin is divided into four parts. I would today divide Ireland into four classes: the landlords, the tenant farmers, the priests and the patriots. I could, doubtless, subdivide each of these classes in four, but the country is so primitive and so barbarous that the first division is quite sufficient. It is even quite complete and in avoiding the extremes, in choosing what seems to me the most typical in each class, I may indicate the principle features which constitute Irish society.] Balzac similarly treats different social groups in rural France in several chapters of *Les Paysans*.

104 Moore's uncle, Joseph Blake, had acted as his agent until 1880.

105 The *Freeman's Journal* was the daily newspaper of moderate nationalists.

106 . . . sans compter le perspective d'un adultère (*Terre*, p. 90) [not counting the prospect of an adultery].

107 . . . un hansom (espèce de cabriolet à deux roues) (*Terre*, p. 90) [a hansom (a type of cabriolet with two wheels)].

108 'or dances in the ballet' and 'and is insatiable as regards the number of her admirers' omitted in *Terre d'Irlande*.

. . . et pour certaines raisons psychologiques fait attendre un mois chacun de ses nouveaux admirateurs. Quand sa vertu s'est assez fait prier, elle avoue qu'elle avait autrefois un ami . . . Cet ami l'a depuis longtemps laissée pour en épouser une autre.

Quoi de plus naturel pour M. Blake que de lui demander qu'il lui soit permis de remplacer cet ami depuis si longtemps perdu? La permission lui est enfin octroyée, et des mois délicieux se passent dans la petite villa de St John's Wood. Mais l'ami perdu a laissé beaucoup de billets non payés. (*Terre*, pp. 90–1) [When her virtue is quite coaxed she claims that she had a friend in the past. This friend left her long ago to marry another. What could be more natural than for Mr Blake to ask her if he would be permitted to replace this long-lost friend? Permission is finally granted and some delicious months are spent in the little house in St John's Wood. But the lost friend has left many unpaid bills.]

109 . . . et à la fin Maud s'aperçoit qu'elle a trop longtemps péché, et commence à parler vertu aux oreilles d'un autre admirateur. (*Terre*, p. 92) [and in the end Maud realises that she has sinned for too long and begins to speak of virtue to the ears of another admirer].

110 'in the Strand' omitted in *Terre d'Irlande*.
. . . à St John's Wood [in St John's Wood].

111 . . . et il soupire après toutes les Maud . . . il lui faut une Maud (*Terre*, p. 94) [and he sighs after every Maud. . . he must have a Maud].

112 'The mother and . . . interest in her.' Omitted in *Terre d'Irlande*.
La mère qui possède une fille passable,—c'est-à-dire une fille dont les jambes soient moins rouges que d'ordinaire, et dont la taille ne ressemble pas tout à fait à un sac de blé, charge les paniers sur le dos de son âne, les remplit de petits poulets, débarbouille sa fille et se dirige vers «la grosse maison».

La mère porte une longue mante de laine noire qu'elle a reçue le jour de ses noces, et qui durera jusqu'à sa mort; elle lui couvre la tête et tombe jusqu'aux chevilles. La fille ne porte ni bonnet ni chapeau; mais si le jour est froid ou s'il fait du vent, elle relève sur sa tête le petit châle jeté sur ses épaules; sa chevelure est bien graissée et légèrement rattachée derrière sa tête par un ruban bleu. Les oies cacardent ou les poules gloussent, selon le cas, dans les paniers; mère et fille attendent, en chuchotant ensemble en irlandais, que le jeune maître sorte. Elles choisisent ordinairement l'heure de midi. Le chien d'arrêt dort sur les marches. Le voilà qui se lève; la mère bat son âne; la jeune fille songe à prendre son air le plus modeste. La porte s'ouvre, et le jeune maître apparaît. Il semble d'abord contrarié, mais dès qu'il aperçoit les joues roses de la jeune fille, il devient plus affable, et demande à voir les volailles; puis après avoir bien reluqué la jeune fille, il paie le prix demandé. (*Terre*, pp. 94–6) [The mother who has a passable daughter, that is to say, a daughter whose legs are less red than usual and whose waist does not wholly resemble a sack of flour, loads the baskets on her donkey's back, fills them with small chickens, scrubs her daughter and sets off to the 'big house'. The mother wears a long black woollen cloak, given to her on her wedding day, and which will last her until her death, it covers her head and falls to her ankles. The daughter wears neither bonnet nor hat, but if the day is cold or windy, she pulls over her head the little black shawl thrown over her shoulders; her hair is very greasy and lightly tied behind her head with a blue ribbon. The geese cackle or the hens cluck, depending on the case, in the baskets; mother and daughter wait, chatting together in Irish, until the young master comes out. They normally choose to come at midday. The pointer is sleeping on the steps. There he is getting up; the mother beats her donkey; the young girl remembers to put on her most modest air. The door opens, and the young man appears. He seems irritated at first, but as soon as he notices the young girl's pink cheeks he becomes more affable, and asks to see the poultry; then having eyed up the young girl, he pays the price asked.]

113   On lui donne des bas épais pour vêtir ses jambes, de fortes bottines pour protéger ses pieds, et un chapeau avec une plume pour aller à l'église. Mais avec tout celà elle ne ressemble pas beaucoup à Maud; cependant, Maud étant devenue impossible, on accepte Biddy. Elle lui donne beaucoup d'enfants, et à mesure que les enfants viennent au monde, les frères de Biddy passent des champs aux étaples; quelques-uns deviennent grooms, baillifs ou garde-chasse. (*Terre*, pp. 96–7) [She is given thick stockings to cover her legs, strong boots to protect her feet, and a hat with a feather to go to church. But with all this, she isn't much like Maud; however, Maud having become impossible, Biddy is acceptable. She gives him many children, and as the children arrive, Biddy's brothers pass from the fields to the stables; some become grooms, bailiffs or gamekeepers.]

114   Mistress Blake entre dans le lit si longtemps et si fructueusement occupé par Biddy. (*Terre*, p. 98) [Mrs Blake enters the bed so long and fruitfully occupied by Biddy.] Frazier tells us that Moore's brother, Maurice Moore, confirmed to Joseph Hone that this story was in fact true, and true of other local gentry and their tenants. Frazier, *George Moore*, p. 141. In *Ave*, Moore reminisces about his friend Dan, who similarly kept a mistress from among his tenants and Dan's brother Mat, who had become religious and sent his mistress, Ellen Ford and their children to America. Moore, *Ave*, pp. 27–31.

115   1877 was the first of three successive seasons of unusually wet and cold weather that afflicted Irish farmers.

116   The first stage in evicting a tenant was the issuing of a notice to quit, or an ejectment order. Sometimes these were not proceeded with as far as eviction but were simply a means of inducing the tenant to pay

the rent. However, evictions rose steeply during the crisis of the early 1880s. In Connacht they increased from 102 net evictions (i.e. eviction numbers minus those readmitted as caretakers) in 1877, to 365 in 1880, 767 in 1881 and 1,430 in 1882. For the country as a whole, there were 5007 families evicted in 1882. T. W. Moody, *Davitt and Irish Revolution, 1846–82* (Oxford, Clarendon, 1981), Appendix D2, p. 564.

117 The date is incorrect. The Land League was founded in 1879.

118 A very large number of evictions occurred during the Great Famine, when landlords used inability to pay rents as an excuse to evict tenants and turn the land over to pasture farming with a smaller number of larger, more solvent tenants. The number evicted is now estimated to have been over half a million people. See Tim P. O'Neill, 'Famine evictions', in Carla King (ed.), *Famine, Land and Culture in Ireland* (Dublin, University College Dublin Press, 2000), pp. 29–70. George Henry Moore had been a model landlord and had not evicted tenants, as his cousin, Lord Sligo, had done. This, however, left his heir, George, with the problem of a property burdened with a large number of insolvent tenants.

119 Moore is here referring to the practice of making provision for allowances to be paid to dependants in landlords' wills. Thus 'the widow' is Mr Blake's mother and 'the younger children' are his siblings.

120 The 1881 Land Act established a Land Commission to arbitrate between landlords and tenants and fix a 'fair rent'. This resulted in reductions in the first five years of between 18 and 20 per cent. After 1886 the reductions were 'almost invariably above 20%, in many cases above 25%'. See Solow, *The Land Question*, p. 174.

121 This was the Tenants' Relief Bill, defeated on 20 September 1886.

122 This was true of the summer of 1886, prior to the declaration of the Plan of Campaign on 20 October, but by the time *Parnell and His Island* in was published in June 1887, the country was once again in crisis.

123 This was a legacy of subdivision, which meant that farms were often composed of dispersed holdings around a locality.

124 This racist caricature is reminiscent of the simian depictions of the Irish in contemporary British magazines such as *Punch*. See Perry L. Curtis, *Apes and Angels: The Irishman in Victorian Caricature* (2nd edn, Washington and London: Smithsonian Institute Press, 1997).

125 'and more ferocious species' omitted in *Terre d'Irlande*.

126 The source of Moore's pseudo-anthropology is unclear. In his day the precursors of the Celts were usually referred to as the Fir-Bolg. Whoever they were, the archaeological record now suggests a level of cultural and economic development in Ireland prior to the Celtic period that is far from Moore's insinuation that these were somehow closer to an anthropoid type. See Michael Herity and George Eogan, *Ireland in*

Prehistory (London and New York: Routledge, 1977); and Gabriel Cooney and Eoin Grogan, *Irish Prehistory: A Social Perspective* (Dublin: Wordwell, 1994).

127 This was no longer the case when Moore was writing. Marriage ages had been low up to the Famine, see Cormac Ó Gráda, *Ireland: A New Economic History 1789–1939* (Oxford: Clarendon, 1994), pp. 7–10. But in the aftermath of the Famine average marriage ages rose, first in the East and later, from the 1870s in the West also. By 1911 Connaught had the lowest marriage rate in Ireland and the latest average age of marriage. See Mary E. Daly, *Social and Economic History of Ireland Since 1800* (Dublin: Educational Company, 1981), pp. 90–2.

128 'and much dull acquiescence . . . providing for it' omitted in *Terre d'Irlande*.

. . . avec cette stupide conviction que Dieu ne fait rien naître à la vie en ce monde sans pourvoir à sa subsistance. (*Terre*, pp. 111–12) [with the stupid conviction that God brings nothing into the world without providing for its means of subsistence.]

129 Elle n'essaie pas de résister, sachant bien que du moment où elle se déclarera enceinte, son père, sa mère, et avant tout le prêtre interviendront. (*Terre*, p. 113) [She does not attempt to resist, knowing well that the moment she declares herself pregnant her father, her mother and above all, the priest will intervene.]

130 Moore appears to be misinformed here. Census figures indicate the number of children born to couples married for less than a year. Of those Irish women marrying in 1910–11 while under 20 years of age, fewer than 13 per cent had babies within the year: while the corresponding figures for England and Wales was 34. See K. H. Connell, *Irish Peasant Society: Four Historical Essays* (Oxford: Oxford University Press, 1968; repr. Dublin: Irish Academic Press, 1996), p. 119. Although this is for a later period than the 1880s, the pattern is unlikely to have been very different for the time Moore described.

131 Elle avait damé le pion à toutes les autres filles; elle avait été séduite; elle allait s'allier au meilleur parti du village, qui sans doute serait forcé de l'épouser (*Terre*, p. 114) [she had got the better of all the other girls; she had been seduced; she would ally herself to the best match in the village, who doubtless would be forced to marry her].

132 . . . la première aventure derrière la meule de foin (*Terre*, p. 115) [the first affair behind the haystack],

133 See Dympna McLoughlin, 'Workhouses and Irish female paupers, 1840–70' in Maria Luddy and Cliona Murphy (eds), *Women Surviving: Studies in Irish Women's History in the Nineteenth and Twentieth Centuries* (Dublin, Poolbeg, 1990), pp. 117–47. Social exclusion and expulsion from the

family home continued in Ireland into the twentieth century. See Myrtle Hill, *Women in Ireland: A Century of Change* (Belfast: Blackstaff, 2003), p. 29.

134 . . . se détachant sur un fond de lac bleu et de montagnes nuageuses (*Terre*, p. 117) [standing out against the blue lake and cloudy mountains].

135 Moore's concern with the plight of the single mother is echoed in the theme of his novel, *Esther Waters* (1894), although the circumstances are different.

136 One of the problems facing tenants like Micky Moran was that the opportunities for earnings from migrant labour were sharply reduced in these years, owing to the agricultural depression affecting British agriculture. See P. J. Perry, *British Farming in the Great Depression, 1840–1914, An Historical Geography* (Newton Abbot: David & Charles, 1974) and Gerard Moran, '"A passage to England": seasonal migration to Britain and post-Famine change in the west of Ireland, 1870–82', *Saothar* XIII (1988): 22–31.

137 Honoré de Balzac, *Études de Mœurs: Scènes de la vie de campagne* vol VIII: *Les Paysans* (1844) ch xii is entitled: 'Le cabaret est le parlement du peuple'. *Les Paysans,* a long, somewhat disconnected novel, is one of the 'Scènes de la vie de campagne' of Balzac's *Comédie humaine*. It turns on the intrigues which in the end drive General de Montcornet to sell his property. The period is *c.*1825; the peasants who engineer the intrigues are the crafty, surly inhabitants of the Morvan, a district in Burgundy. See Harvey and Heseltine, *Oxford Companion to French Literature*, p. 545.

138 . . . fils de putin (*Terre*, p. 123) [son of a whore]

139 Tenants who took over land from which others had been evicted were particular objects of resentment, boycotting and occasionally violence, in the Irish countryside.

140 Mrs Page: 'Well, I will find you twenty lascivious turtles ere one chaste man'. Shakespeare, *The Merry Wives of Windsor*, Act 2 Scene 1.

141 'other immorality' given in *Terre* as 'la fornication', (p. 131).

142 On dit qu'on leur fait boire à Maynooth pendant deux ans du bromure de potassium; ici les documents me font défaut; mais s'il est vrai qu'on n'ait pas recours à pareilles précautions, je ne connais pas de plus interessant sujet de roman que l'histoire d'un homme qui avait péché avant l'époque de sa prêtrise, et qui fut suivi dans la solitude de sa paroisse par la jeune fille qu'il avait séduite. (*Terre*, pp. 131–2) [It is said that during two years at Maynooth they are made to drink potassium bromide; I have no documents to prove this; but if it is true that they do not have recourse to some similar precautions, I don't know of a more interesting subject for a novel than the story of a man who had sinned before the time of his priesthood and who was followed into the

solitude of his parish by the young girl he had seduced]. It is possible that we see here the germ of Moore's later novel, *The Lake*.

143 Clerical celibacy was a theme that interested Moore. In his novel *The Lake* (1905) his story centred on an Irish priest, Father Oliver Gogarty, who falls in love with one of his parishioners.

144 The Roman Catholic priesthood played an important role in local nationalist politics in the 1880s and 1890s. See Emmet Larkin, *The Roman Catholic Church and the Plan of Campaign in Ireland, 1886–1888* (Cork: Cork University Press, 1978).

145 As a child Moore was himself tutored by such a priest. Father James Browne, parish priest of Carnacun, tutored him in the Classics in 1864, when he had been sent home from Oscott with a lung infection. See Frazier, *George Moore*, pp. 14–15.

146 'assassination' omitted in *Terre d'Irlande*, replaced with 'boycotting' (p. 35).

147 See Joyce Marlowe, *Captain Boycott and the Irish* (London: Deutsch, 1973).

148 'the leader writer' 'assassination' given in *Terre* as
. . . des meilleurs écrivains [the best writers] (p. 138).

149 This account resembles that of the Bartons' Mass going in *A Drama in Muslin*, pp. 68–72.

150 'the new action of Ireland to-day' omitted in *Terre d'Irlande*.
. . . les idées nouvelles et la révolution du jour (p. 139) [new ideas and the revolution of the day].

151 This is a veiled reference to the anticlerical traditions of the Fenians.

152 On the close relationship between Irish Catholic priests and rural shopkeepers, see Líam Kennedy, 'The early response of the Irish Catholic clergy to the Co-operative Movement', *Irish Historical Studies* XXI, 81 (March 1978): 55–74.

153 Cattle trough.

154 Lemon verbena.

155 'his murmuring' given in *Terre* as
. . . son jeu (p. 145) [his game].

156 Here Father Tom is trying to make a distinction between religion and politics which his parishioners are unwilling to accept.

157 To keep both sides sweet. Literally: 'to handle the goat and the cabbages'. '. . . le chou' in *Terre* (p. 148).

158 The mutilation of cattle, in order to punish their owner by reducing their market value, was a frequent occurrence during the land war, despite its denunciation by the leadership of the land movement.

159 There was no *Clare Telegraph:* this is likely to have been an allusion to the *Connaught Telegraph*. See Introduction, p. xix.

160 Once again, Moore has mistaken the date of the foundation of the Land League. It was 1879.

161 The real James Daly (see Introduction, p. xix) was an important figure in local politics before the founding of the Land League, which he spearheaded, together with a group of Mayo and Galway activists. In 1876 he became an owner of the *Connaught Telegraph* and was its editor until 1888. Davitt became involved in the land movement early in 1879 but Parnell only committed himself to it in the autumn of 1879. See Gerard Moran, 'James Daly and the rise and fall of the Land League in the west of Ireland, 1879–82', *Irish Historical Studies* XXIX, 114 (Nov. 1994), pp. 189–207.

162 The real James Daly was asked by Parnell to contest either Sligo or Leitrim for the Home Rule Party at the 1880 election but refused, saying that he would have nothing to do with the House of Commons. He remained, however, an important local and national figure. See Moran, 'James Daly', p. 198.

163 Euston Station is to this day the London terminus of the railway link from the Dun Laoghaire to Holyhead ferry.

164 Lambeth was a relatively poor part of London. In *Terre d'Irlande*, it is cited as Pimlico.

165 . . . pendant que la chair se refroidit et a faim [while his flesh cools and hungers].

166 'although they appear . . . bewitching' omitted in *Terre d'Irlande*.
. . . mais il lui semble impossible qu'il y ait un mortel assez heureux pour les posséder; à ses yeux elles sont merveilleusement habillées, elles sont belles, elles sont ravissantes; ce sont des reines. (p. 158) [but it seems impossible that there is a mortal in the happy situation to possess them; in his eyes they are wonderfully dressed, they are beautiful, they are delightful, they are queens.]

167 'he dare not yet aspire to be one of that gay throng' omitted in *Terre d'Irlande.*
. . . il ne saurait dire qui est la prostituée et qui est la lady; si quelque hasard détermine son choix, il ne peut formuler son désir en paroles; il est abasourdi, confondu, plein de perplexité; il ne sait pas combien d'argent il faut offrir; puis il a entendu raconter des histoires de maladie et de vol (*Terre*, p. 160) [he cannot say which is the prostitute and which is the lady; if some accident determines his choice, he cannot put his wish into words; he is stunned, confounded, perplexed; he doesn't know how much money one should offer; then he has heard tell of disease and theft].

168 Mais ses plaisirs ne se bornent pas là. Au bout d'une semaine il est accosté par une forte et plantureuse femme aux joues rouges—une femme ressemblant à une servante hors d'emploi—précisément la femme

après laquelle il soupirait, lorsqu'il vit ces délicates créatures en fourrure et en soie blanche sortir du restaurant à la mode dans Regent Street. Jusqu'alors ses amours s'étaient consommées dans un champ fangeux au milieu des bouses de vache, derrière les remparts de la ville du comté, avec des mendiantes et des vagabondes qu'on ne saurait nommer ni concevoir, ou avec d'affreuses mégères qui l'attiraient dans quelque coin noir de Merrion Square: se sentir dans un lit, entre deux draps, avec une femme propre et solide, c'était donc un indicible bonheur, une vive et insondable jouissance pour cet Irlandais primitif, une satisfaction sans entraves à ses vigoureux et ardents instincts. Les souvenirs de cette nuit sont comme un sucre dans sa bouche; son coeur et sa chair avides aspirent à une nouvelle extase et à de nouveaux ébattements. (*Terre*, pp. 161–2) [But his pleasures do not end there. After a week he is accosted by a strong, well-built woman with red cheeks—a woman who resembles an out-of-work servant—precisely the kind of woman he sighed for when he saw those delicate creatures in fur and white silk leaving the fashionable restaurant in Regent Street. Until then his loves had been consummated in a muddy field among the cow pats, behind the walls of the county town with beggars and tramps who one could neither name nor imagine, or with the awful shrews who enticed him in some black corner of Merrion Square. To be in a bed, between two curtains, with a clean, sturdy woman, this was an inexpressible happiness, a lively and unfathomable joy for this primitive Irishman, a satisfaction without hindrance to his strong and passionate instincts. The memories of this night are like sugar in the mouth, his heart and his avid flesh aspire to a new ecstasy and to new frolics.]

169 What Moore is snobbishly alluding to is the fact that the Irish representation had altered in its social composition in the course of the 1870s, and was no longer the preserve of landlords and the upper middle class that it had been until then. See David Thornley, *Isaac Butt and Home Rule* (London: MacGibbon & Kee, 1964), p. 207.

170 'the streets will be empty' omitted in *Terre d'Irlande*.

. . . il n'y aura pas une femme dans la rue quand la Chambre se séparera, pas une! (*Terre*, p. 163) [there won't be a woman left when the House breaks up—not one!]

171 . . . elles sont toutes à cette forte femme qui bat son quart près de Westminster Bridge. Quelque autre l'aura ramassée; elle sera rentrée chez elle (*Terre*, p. 163) [they are all with that large woman who keeps her beat on Westminster Bridge. Someone else will have picked her up; she will have returned home].

172 'the cheap eating-house' omitted in *Terre d'Irlande*.

. . . les prostituées de Westminster Bridge (*Terre*, p. 164) [the prostitutes of Westminster Bridge].

173 Funding from Irish-Americans provided a new and important weapon in the land war. The amount sent to the Land League from the United States came to over one million dollars in the three years from 1880 to 1883 but much of this money was used for famine relief and assistance to evicted tenants. In the seven years until 1890, an additional million dollars came from the Irish in America. Arnold Schrier, *Ireland and the American Emigration, 1850–1900* (2nd edn, Chester Springs PA: Dufour, 1997), p. 128.

174 In *Terre d'Irlande* this chapter is called 'Un Château Mort' [A Dead Castle]. In *Terre d'Irlande* the chapter, 'Une Éviction' is placed before 'Un Château Mort'.

175 Castle Burke, alias Kilvoynell Castle stands in ruins close to Lough Carra. It was a MacEvilly (Staunton) stronghold. See Michael Morris, Lord Killanin and Michael V. Duignan, *The Shell Guide to Ireland* (3rd edn, Dublin: Gill & Macmillan, 1989), p. 87.

176 The lake is Lough Carra, which Moore Hall overlooks. It has an area of 4,000 acres and is approximately six miles long.

177 Brendan Fleming suggests that the image of the stormy lake should be read as a counterpoint to the opening scene of the book: 'Its turbulence shatters the enchanted calm and stillness the narrator imposed on Dublin Bay at the opening of the text. There, the water's mirror-like qualities symbolized the text's ability to reflect Irish experience. This is now no longer feasible. The mirror has become cracked and fragmented' (p. 74). 'French spectacles in an Irish case: From "Lettres sur l'Irlande" to *Parnell and His Island*', in Alan A. Gillis and Aaron Kelly (eds), *Critical Ireland: New Essays in Literature and Culture* (Dublin: Four Courts, 2001), pp. 69–76.

178 . . . le travail, le travail . . . la meilleur des opiats! (*Terre*, p. 206) [work, work . . . the best of opiates].

179 Castle Carra was built some time between 1238 and 1300 by de Staunton, one of the Anglo-Norman barons in the following of Richard de Burgo. The present remains consist of a three-storied tower standing in a strongly fortified bawn with one rounded corner turret. Much of the present building would appear to be of fifteenth-century date, but it undoubtedly incorporates older fragments. The family who built it later took on the name of McEvilly, and held it until at least 1574. Some time after this the castle was surrendered to the crown and granted to Captain William Bowen, whose family kept it until the Cromwellian period. After the Restoration in 1660 it was granted to Sir Henry Lynch, in whose family it remained until the nineteenth century. See Peter Harbison, *Guide to the National and Historic Monuments of Ireland* (Dublin: Gill & Macmillan, 1970, 1992), p. 245.

180 . . . et nous appelons le jour de tous nos vœux (*Terre*, p. 208) [and we call up the day with full voices].

181 Mon front est moite de la rosée de la tombe, ma chair et mon sang sont aussi froids que cette lueur blanche. (*Terre*, p. 211) [My brow is damp from the dew of the tomb, my skin and my blood are as cold as this white glimmer].

182 Brendan Fleming suggests that this encounter may be read as a metaphor for the threat posed by 'Captain Moonlight' to landlordism. Fleming, 'French spectacles', p. 73.

183 'gaunt castle' given in *Terre* as
. . . squelette décharné . . . (p. 212) [gaunt skeleton]

184 . . . la terreur n'a point encore déjelé dans mes os (*Terre*, p. 213) [. . . the terror has not yet quite thawed from my bones].

185 This is Castle Burke, referred to above.

186 In *Terre d'Irlande* this chapter is entitled 'Un château vivant'.

187 This is Ashford Castle, the neo-Gothic castle constructed by Lord and Lady Ardilaun near Cong.

188 'as the jolting-car . . . to stay with' omitted in *Terre d'Irlande*.
Pendant que nous sommes cahotés dans la voiture à travers ce misérable pays de fondrières noires, de rocs gris et de montagnes bleues, ayant toujours sous les yeux ce même spectacle: sordides huttes baignant dans l'humidité d'un champ de pommes de terre, chaumières en ruines racontant l'histoire de leurs habitants expulsés, longs bois cachant les blanches maisons carrées des propriétaires, nous causons des gens que nous allons voir. (*Terre*, p. 220) [As we are jolted in the car across this miserable country of black potholes, grey rocks and blue mountains, having the same view always in our eyes: sordid huts, bathing in the damp of a potato field, cottages in ruins telling the story of their evicted inhabitants, long woods hiding the square white houses of the land-owners, we chat about the people we are going to see.]

189 Lord Ardilaun received £680,000 for his share in Guinness's brewery. See Patrick Lynch and John Vaizey, *Guinness's Brewery in the Irish Economy* (Cambridge: Cambridge University Press, 1960) p. 193.

190 . . . sous les opulents ombrages des tropiques (*Terre*, p. 221) [under the rich shade of the tropics]. Sir Arthur Edward Guinness (later Lord Ardilaun) completed work which his father had begun in reconstructing Archbishop Marsh's Library near St Patrick's Cathedral in Dublin. He rebuilt the Coombe Lying-in Hospital, became chairman of the first Dublin organisation to concern itself with the housing of artisans, and served for 16 years as the President of the Royal Dublin Society. In 1880 he was raised to the peerage as Baron Ardilaun of Ashford. See Lynch and Vaizey, *Guiness's Brewery*, p. 196.

191 Lord Ardilaun inherited a very large estate at Ashford, County Galway. There he undertook extensive afforestation, providing employment to one of the more impoverished parts of Connemara. He also boosted the tourist industry in the West by maintaining a steamer service on Lough Corrib between Ashford Castle, Cong and Galway City.

192 Théophile Gautier (1811–72) was a major French poet, novelist, dramatist and critic, whose novel, *Mlle de Maupin*, had an early influence on Moore. See Moore, *Confessions of a Young Man*, pp. 66–7, 68, 70.

193 'it' given in *Terre* as

. . . le parti extrême (p. 225) . . . [the extremists]

194 'long shadowy saloon . . . moon' omitted in *Terre d'Irlande*.

. . . dans la grande chambre gothique, où je fais ma toilette devant un haut miroir entre deux chandelles brillant comme des étoiles perdues dans l'ombre, je m'arrête à contempler la lune (p. 227) [In the great Gothic chamber, where I dress before a high mirror between two candles, shining like stars lost in the darkness, I stop to look at the moon . . .].

195 Percy Bysshe Shelley (1792–1822) was a Romantic poet. Moore had been deeply impressed by Shelley's poetry while still a schoolboy. Even when he first went to Paris in 1873, he recollects that Shelley was 'still my "pinnace"'. Moore, *Confessions of a Young Man*, p. 60.

196 . . . les projets pour l'emploi de la journée. . . (*Terre*, p. 229) [projects for day's schedule]

197 . . . puis après la conversation, le cigare, la flânerie dans la faisanderie, et la visite aux chenils (*Terre*, p. 229) [then afterwards, a conversation, a cigar, a stroll in the pheasantry, and a visit to the kennels . . .]

198 'For as we sit at breakfast' omitted in *Terre d'Irlande*.

Quand nous cherchons un abri contre la pluie sous les voûtes de l'abbaye en ruines qui domine la rivière (*Terre*, p. 229) [While we are seeking shelter from the rain under the vaults of the ruined abbey which dominates the river . . .]

199 'and sometimes' given in *Terre* as

Un jour de lunch au château . . . (p. 230) [one day during lunchtime at the castle]

200 'breakfast' replaced by lunch in *Terre d'Irlande*.

201 This is the island of Inchagoill.

202 There seems to be a hint at a lesbian relationship between Miss Barrett and Miss McCoy, a theme also touched upon in *A Drama in Muslin* in the character of Cecilia Cullen.

203 Combien d'agneaux avez-vous châtrés cette année? Combien de marcassins avez-vous coupés? (*Terre*, p. 171) [How many lambs have you castrated this year? How many boars have you gelded?]

204 'founding a convent' omitted in *Terre d'Irlande*.

. . . entrer au couvent (*Terre*, p. 173) [entering a convent].

205 . . . l'âcre puanteur des pots de chambre non vidés laissés sur le passage vous prend au nez (*Terre*, p. 175) [the acrid stench of the un-emptied chamber pots left on the passage assails your nostrils].

206 'she goes down . . . in the fold.' omitted in *Terre d'Irlande*.

. . . mieux encore, elle assiste le berger pendant qu'il châtre les agneaux et quelquefois c'est à qui d'elle ou de lui fera le plus grand nombre d'opérations dans un espace de temps donné.

Discutant le prix d'un taureau à une foire, on l'a entendue déprécier les parties sexuelles de l'animal et répondre au propriétaire qui soutenait qu'elle se trompait: «Hé bien, alors, faites-lui faire un tour jusqu'à ce que je le sente.» Et cela dit de bonne foi, sans aucune arrière-pensée. (*Terre*, p. 177) [better still, she helps the shepherd when he castrates the lambs and sometimes it is a moot point whether she or he carries out the greatest number of operations in the given time. When discussing the price of a bull at a fair one hears her disparaging the private parts of the animal and replying to the owner who maintains that she is mistaken, 'Well then, make him turn around so that I can feel it.' And all this is said in good faith, without any ulterior motive.]

207 Castlebar.

208 These seem to be misprints in the original for Kiltimach and Claremorris. In *Terre* the towns are given as de Loughrea, de Ballinafad, de Catheriney, de Claremorris, de Kelimach.

209 . . . de Slego [from Sligo].

210 Logafoil seems to have been a hamlet near Castlebar, County Mayo.

211 'gaunt hungry Scotchwoman' given in *Terre* as

. . . squelette ambulant (p. 180) [walking skeleton]

212 . . . putain [whore]

213 'of a like delicate nature,' given in *Terre* as

. . . à la castration des agneaux [to the castration of lambs]. . . (p. 181)

214 La porte de la misérable habitation est barricadée (*Terre*, p. 184) [the door of the miserable house is barricaded].

215 Billeen/Bilín—little Billy; sollach/salach—dirty, obscene.

216 'brings in a saucepan of milk' omitted in *Terre d'Irlande*.

. . . met les piets dans une casserole de lait . . . (*Terre*, p. 190) [a neighbour steps in a pot of milk . . .].

217 Awornine/a mhuirnín—dear.

218 'Dans un endroit indécent' (*Terre*, p. 190) [In an indecent place]

219 Stopping the hunt was a tactic used by the tenant side in the Land War as a form of passive resistance against landlords. Anthony Trollope also described it in his novel, *The Landleaguers* (1881).

220 Athenry in *Terre d'Irlande*.

221 This was Empress Elizabeth of Austria (1837–98). She visited Ireland twice, in 1879 and 1880. She was assassinated by an Italian anarchist, while on a visit to Switzerland, in September 1898.

222 Mistress Jack est une véritable sauvage; son esprit n'a jamais subi la moindre influence civilisatrice; elle n'a jamais lu un seul livre de sa vie; elle peut avoir entendu dire que Shakespeare est un poète, mais je suis sûr qu'elle n'a jamais entendu parler de Milton ni de Lord Byron, et qu'elle n'a jamais lu un roman de Thackeray ou de Dickens. Je me souviens qu'un jour elle prit une photographie de Beethoven et me demanda qui il était. «Ne savez-vous pas, lui dis-je, que Beethoven c'est le grand éléveur de bêtes à cornes.» «Et quel est cet autre? dit-elle.»

«Oh! celui-ci, c'est Wagner, Richard Wagner, le grand éléveur de poneys.»

«Je m'étonne fort, répliqua-t-elle, que je ne l'ai jamais rencontré à la foire des chevaux à Dublin. (*Terre*, p. 244) [Mistress Jack is a real savage; her spirit has never been subjected to the least civilising influence; she has never read a single book in her life; she may have heard that Shakespeare is a poet, but I am certain that she has never heard tell of Milton or Lord Byron, and that she never read a novel by Thackeray or Dickens. I remember one day she picked up a photograph of Beethoven and asked me who it was. 'Do you not know,' I said to her, 'that Beethoven is a great livestock breeder.'

'And who is this other one?' she said.

'Oh, that one, that's Wagner, Richard Wagner, the great pony breeder.'

'I'm very surprised,' she replied, 'that I never met him at the horse fair in Dublin'.] If this character was based on Maud Browne's aunt, he was cruelly satirising his own relative here. Maud's mother and Moore's mother were Blakes, but there were four Blake sisters and which one was the 'ogress' is not clear. See Frazier, *George Moore*, pp. 103, 496 n.44.

223 This character is believed to be based on Maud Browne, Moore's cousin, with whom he had a brief but unsuccessful courtship in early 1884.

224 Mashing—flirting with.

225 Squanders—leaves behind

226 Whips assist the Master of Hounds in managing the hunt.

227 Moore is here describing the village of Southwick, near Brighton, where he was writing this. He also depicts the village in his novel *Spring Days* (1888).

228 One is as good as the other.

229   Here we seem to have an echo of the Impressionists' view of representation in art. Moore appears to suggest that he is trying in words to achieve what they aimed at in painting.

230   Parnell's explanation of moonlighting that it was the only preventive against eviction was mistakenly used to suggest that he approved of it. He was sometimes depicted as 'Captain Moonlight' in cartoons in the 1880s.

231   'Parisian, Jovian, or Christian' omitted in *Terre d'Irlande*.

232   Moore is referring here to the operation of the Land Commission under the 1881 Land Act which fixed what were considered to be 'fair rents'.

233   Ils sont soixante-dix (*Terre*, p. 266) [there are seventy of them]. This is a reference to the payment of an allowance of MPs adopted by the National party in March 1884 and put into effect after the 1885 election.

234   The problem that faced Irish farmers was that agricultural prices had continued to fall during the depression and many were unable to pay even the reduced rents. In 1886 the value of agricultural output was only 64 per cent of its 1876 level. See Solow, *The Land Question*, pp. 171–3.

235   On 6 May 1882 the Chief Secretary for Ireland, Lord Frederick Cavendish and his undersecretary, Thomas Burke, were assassinated outside the Viceregal Lodge in Phoenix Park. The attack was carried out by the Invincibles, a splinter group of the Irish Republican Brotherhood.

236   The Prevention of Crimes Act was passed on 12 July 1882.

237   I have been unable to trace this incident [ed.].

238   On 18 August 1882 five members of the family of John Joyce were murdered at Maamtrasna, County Galway. Three men were executed, five sentenced to penal servitude for life for the murders. See Jarlath Waldron, *Maamtrasna: The Murders and the Mystery* (Dublin: Edmund Burke, 1992).

239   On 11 December 1883, Parnell was presented with a testimonial of over £37,000.

240   The belief that if a tenant was seen to make any investment in his holding the landlord or agent would immediately raise the rent was often cited as a disincentive to agricultural improvement.

241   . . . et executions agraires [and agrarian executions].

242   Balzac, *Les Paysans*, ch. xiii. There was a great deal of concern in the 1880s over rural indebtedness. In 1881 the Report of the Royal Commission into the Depressed Condition of the Agricultural Interest (Richmond Commission) drew attention to the problem of rural indebtedness in Ireland. This may be seen as an effect of the commercialisation of the rural economy that took place in the decades following the Famine,

coupled with the effects of a sudden downturn in agricultural incomes as a result of bad harvests and the onset of the agricultural depression.

243 Moore is here referring to the teachings of the Land League and its successor, the National League.

244 He is referring here to the Home Rule Party's tactic of parliamentary obstruction.

245 Moore's meaning is not entirely clear here, but he may refer to the fact that Irish votes had by 1887 overthrown a Liberal government on 9 June 1885 and a Conservative government on 28 January 1886, while Gladstone's efforts to legislate for Home Rule resulted in a Liberal defeat in the elections of July 1886.

246 'and a cheap dinner, for—let us say' omitted in *Terre d'Irlande*.

247 Randolph Henry Spencer, Lord Churchill (1849–95) had taken a leading role in opposition to W. E. Gladstone's 1886 Home Rule Bill. In the general election of July 1886, the Liberal government was defeated and the Conservatives returned to government, led by Lord Salisbury. In a speech as Leader of the House of Commons, on 19 August 1886, Churchill asserted the new government's determination to uphold the Union.

248 Robert Arthur Talbot Gascoyne-Cecil, third Marquess of Salisbury (1830–1902), served as Conservative Prime Minister in 1885–6, 1886–92 and 1895–1902.

249 John Morley (1838–1923), a well-known journalist, intellectual and Radical politician. Morley entered Parliament in 1883, serving as Irish Chief Secretary in 1886 and in 1892–5.

250 As the Russian Empire expanded into Central Asia in the mid-nineteenth century, it was seen as a potential threat to British interests in northern India. In October 1879 British forces occupied Kabul and forced the abdication of its ruler, Yakub Khan, and installed Abdurrahman Khan in his place. In early 1885 a serious Anglo-Russian crisis occurred when on 30 March Russian troops clashed with Afghan forces at Penjdeh and it was thought that they intended to advance still further into the area. However, they had no serious desire to expand further at this time and in May a preliminary agreement was made on conditions for arbitration of the frontier dispute. This was formally agreed on 15 September 1885. See Hugh Seton-Watson, *The Russian Empire, 1801–1917* (Oxford: Clarendon: 1967, 1990), pp. 569–70 and A. J. P. Taylor, *The Struggle for Mastery in Europe, 1848–1918* (London: Oxford University Press, 1977), pp. 298–301.